DANIKA COOLEY

60 SCRIPTURES YOU CAN PRAY

Going to God's Word for
Guidance, Deliverance, Thanksgiving, and More

WHITAKER
HOUSE

60 Scriptures You Can Pray
Going to God's Word for Guidance, Deliverance, Thanksgiving, and More

DanikaCooley.com

ISBN: 979-8-88769-608-9 | eBook ISBN: 979-8-88769-609-6
Printed in the United States of America

Whitaker House | 1030 Hunt Valley Circle | New Kensington, PA 15068
www.whitakerhouse.com

Library of Congress Cataloging-in-Publication Data
Names: Cooley, Danika author
Title: 60 scriptures you can pray : going to God's word for guidance, deliverance, thanksgiving, and more / Danika Cooley.
Other titles: Sixty scriptures you can pray
Description: New Kensington, PA : Whitaker House, [2026] | Summary: "Suggests Scripture verses that believers can use to pray to God, under the themes of praise, thanksgiving, confession, supplication, intercession, deliverance, lament, and guidance, to develop a daily prayer habit and discover how to pray biblically"— Provided by publisher.
Identifiers: LCCN 2025032514 (print) | LCCN 2025032515 (ebook) | ISBN 9798887696089 trade paperback | ISBN 9798887696096 ebook
Subjects: LCSH: Bible—Prayers | Prayer—Christianity | BISAC: RELIGION / Christian Living / Prayer | RELIGION / Biblical Meditations / General
Classification: LCC BS680.P64 C66 2026 (print) | LCC BS680.P64 (ebook)
LC record available at https://lccn.loc.gov/2025032514
LC ebook record available at https://lccn.loc.gov/2025032515

1 2 3 4 5 6 7 8 9 10 11 WH 33 32 31 30 29 28 27 26

HERE'S WHAT PEOPLE ARE SAYING ABOUT DANIKA COOLEY AND *60 SCRIPTURES YOU CAN PRAY*

Eight minutes. It occurs to me that if you invest that much time each day for two months in Danika Cooley's thoughtfully crafted devotional, you'll find yourself praying the exact words spoken by dozens of real people who lived the Bible—Peter, David, Hannah, Mary, Paul, Job, Hagar, Elisha, Esther, Joel, Jabez, Deborah, and many more. What a blessing! Just don't be surprised if eight minutes turns into thirty ... or into a lifetime of praying without ceasing.

—*Jay Payleitner*
Best-selling author, *52 Things Kids Need from a Dad; What If God Wrote Your Bucket List?*

What a treasure! *60 Scriptures You Can Pray* by Danika Cooley offers a breath of Scripture-infused fresh air—a user-friendly blend of practical encouragement, winsome challenges, and inspiring biblical truth. This devotional will be a valued go-to for anyone seeking a deeper daily conversation with the Lord.

—*Robert Elmer*
Editor, *Prayers of the Church* series

Have you noticed that your prayers tend to follow the same familiar paths? You feel sure that talking with God can be more personal and vibrant, but you are not sure how to get there. Danika Cooley's *60 Scriptures You Can Pray* follows the time-tested method of using Bible prayers as patterns according to which we can make other prayers that correspond to our own circumstances. *60 Scriptures* will help you understand a rich variety of biblical prayers through which your believing ancestors invite you to *"Pray then like this"* (Matthew 6:9). This book strengthened my prayerfulness as well as my family's. If you want to advance in this essential spiritual discipline, ask Jesus, *"Lord, teach us to pray"* (Luke 11:1) and use this book to gain insights into His answer.

—*William Boekestein*
Author; pastor of Immanuel Fellowship Church

Many struggle with the discipline of prayer. Danika Cooley has approached this issue from a fresh and innovative direction. You will find scriptural and practical encouragement from this excellent new resource.

—*Brook Wayne*
Cofounder, FamilyRenewal.org

CONTENTS

Prayers of Intercession

Prayers for Deliverance

Prayers of Lament

Prayers for Guidance

INTRODUCTION
PRAY LIKE THIS

God's people are a praying people. My husband, Ed, and I were young in the faith Christians when we first began to pray that God's kingdom would come and His will would be done, here on earth as it is in heaven. We didn't think of our prayers that way initially.

Instead, we gradually noticed that, on an average grocery store trip, we passed several sex shops, pagan temples, and fortune tellers. Scripture tells us these things grieve God's heart, and they began to grieve ours as well. So as we drove, we appealed aloud to the God of the universe, "Lord, we know this place is an affront to Your holiness. Please close it and bring the people there to salvation in You."

A couple of months after we began praying, Ed and I drove past a familiar prominent house with a stained-glass door featuring a life-sized wizard. Workmen were removing both the door and the large wooden sign advertising the services of a medium. I was shocked. God heard, and He answered.

As we kept praying, shops and temples continued to close. When we moved to a new town over a dozen years later, one large strip club remained just blocks from our old home. One morning, I asked the Lord why He allowed the joint to remain. Later that day, I read a news article about two young girls who had been trafficked from that same club during the years we had been praying. They turned eighteen, sued the management, and won. Today that building houses a Korean barbecue restaurant.

The Bible prayers in this book were prayed to a very real God by real people facing real joy, danger, and heartache. God's Word is full of prayer to our amazing God—and it records His answers. During His Sermon on the Mount, Jesus said:

> *Pray then like this: "Our Father in heaven, hallowed be your name. Your kingdom come, your will be done, on earth as it is in heaven. Give us this day our daily bread, and forgive us our debts, as we also have forgiven our debtors. And lead us not into temptation, but deliver us from evil."*
>
> (Matthew 6:9–13)

Jesus gave us a framework for prayer. We are to praise our Father God and to seek His will here, even as we look forward to eternity with Him. We petition God for our needs and repent of our sins. We pray on behalf of others and ask God to deliver us from evil.

God's Word records many different types of prayer. You will explore eight types in this book:

- Praise: We adore God for who He is.
- Thanksgiving: We worship God for what He has done.
- Confession: We repent and admit our sin, both for salvation and for our daily sins.

- Supplication: We ask God to meet our own needs and to strengthen us to serve Him.
- Intercession: We petition God on behalf of others.
- Deliverance: In times of danger, we ask God to save us.
- Lament: We bring our pain to God.
- Guidance: We ask God for His sovereign direction in our lives.

Because the sixty Bible prayers are divided into these sections, you can work through this devotional in order, or you can skip straight to the section that speaks loudest to your current circumstances.

Over the next couple days, look up a few verses *about* prayer. Start with Romans 8:26, 12:12, and 1 Thessalonians 5:16–18. Consider beginning a journal to record your prayers and keep track of how God answers them.

PRAYERS OF PRAISE

Stand up and praise the L*ORD* *your God, for he lives from everlasting to everlasting!*

—Nehemiah 9:5 NLT

We adore God for who He is.

DAY 1

TO THE LORD I WILL SING

Hear, O kings; give ear, O princes; to the Lord *I will sing;*
I will make melody to the Lord, *the God of Israel.*

(Judges 5:3)

Read: Judges 5:1–9, 31

Do you ever wonder if there will be a battle in the streets outside your front door today? Probably not. Our modern problems are just as real as those experienced by people in the Old Testament, but they tend to be a bit less violent. Yet through all of life's challenges, God is our friend.

In the days of Israel's judges, peace was elusive, and the people lived in an ongoing cycle of apostasy, during which they turned from God and committed evil acts. First, they ceased to be faithful to their God. Then, because of their spiritual rebellion, God allowed other nations to oppress the Israelites. Eventually, the women and men of Israel cried out to God for help. Finally, God mercifully sent a judge to help save His people from destruction. After following the Lord for a period of time, the people lived out the cycle all over again.

During the fourth cycle of apostasy, God gave the people over to Jabin, the king of Canaan. Jabin, in turn, set his army commander, Sisera, over the Israelites. The people lived for twenty years in misery under the cruel Sisera and his massive army, which included nine hundred chariots.

During that time, God provided a godly married mother, Deborah, as a prophetess and judge. Deborah would sit under a tree and judge the people's troubles. One day, Deborah asked the warrior Barak why he had declined God's call to lead men from the tribes of Naphtali and Zebulun against Sisera's army. Barak responded that he refused to lead God's people unless Deborah went with him.

Deborah replied that she would accompany Barak, but that meant the victory would go to a woman. So Barak, Deborah, and ten thousand men marched toward Mount Tabor to meet Sisera and his army. While Sisera's army fell to Israelite swords, another woman, Jael, killed Sisera as he slept, ending the Canaanite occupation of Israel's tribes.

After God gave Deborah and Jael victory over Sisera, Deborah sang a prayer of praise to the Lord. She detailed the story of God's mercy toward Israel, ending with, *"So may all your enemies perish, O Lord! But your friends be like the sun as he rises in his might"* (Judges 5:31). Isn't that a wonderful prayer? May we be friends with the Lord. May we be like the sun—strong and unwavering in our love of the Lord and His ways.

Unlike Old Testament battles, our modern-day victories often involve struggles with the monthly budget, the broken washing machine, and the children who refuse to eat dinner. When we manage to spend each day in service to God and to the people around us, that is a real victory. We can praise God for giving us strength to be faithful to our true love, Jesus.

Pray: *Father, thank You for peace in my neighborhood today. Help me to be faithful in serving You each day and help me remember to come to You with my needs. Praise You for making me Your friend. Let my song always be to You alone.*

DAY 2

MY HEART REJOICES IN THE LORD

There is none holy like the Lord: for there is none besides you; there is no rock like our God. (1 Samuel 2:2)

Read: 1 Samuel 2:1–10

Do you ever look around and wonder if everything just happens by chance? While it can seem like our circumstances are random, the Bible tells us that God is the one who commands heaven's armies. He is sovereign over the events of our lives as well.

The book of 1 Samuel begins with the story of Hannah, whom God kept from conceiving a child. Even in her painful situation, Hannah knew it is the Lord who opens and closes wombs. So Hannah prevailed on God to give her a child. When God did indeed grant Hannah a boy, she entrusted her toddler son to the care of Eli the priest, saying, *"I prayed for this child, and the Lord has granted me what I asked of him. So now I give him to the Lord"* (1 Samuel 1:27–28 NIV). Hannah's son, Samuel, grew up to lead the nation of Israel as God's servant and prophet.

In her initial prayer, Hannah referred to God as the *"Lord of Heaven's Armies"* (1 Samuel 1:11 NLT). Later, Hannah praised God as sovereign over all things. (See 1 Samuel 2:1–10.) The word *sovereign* means the supreme authority. That's just what God is: the supreme commander of the heavenly armies, worthy of our praise.

In her long prayer, Hannah praised God as holy and as uniquely God. The Lord is our rock and our solid ground. He knows and judges our hearts, not just our actions. The Lord of armies rules over all circumstances, humbling the mighty and strengthening the weak. For His own purposes, our God gives or withholds food, the sustenance of life.

Hannah knew that God satisfies us in our families and preserves our children as they grow into adulthood. God is sovereign over life and death and over heaven and hell too. After all, *"Salvation belongs to the Lord"* (Psalm 3:8). God gives and takes wealth and status, and He rescues those He chooses from poverty and dishonor. God cares for those who follow and love Him, but those who mock God will regret their foolishness.

Hannah found herself in a tough position. She was one of two wives, loved by her husband but taunted by his other spouse. Unable to bear children, she felt her loss deeply. Yet Hannah knew that God is sovereign over all, and she went straight to Him with her most important request. God chose to bless Hannah with an influential, godly son, followed by another three sons and two daughters.

It may seem terrifying to acknowledge that God is the ruler of all things, including wombs, checkbooks, and salvation. Our God, though, is good and holy, just and righteous. We can trust Him. Romans 8:28 reminds us, *"We know that for those who love God all things work together for good, for those who are called according to his purpose."*

Pray: *Lord, my heart rejoices in You and in Your salvation. You determine the length of our lives and our position here on earth. No one who is against You will prevail. I will remember Your goodness to me, even when Your answer to my prayer is "no" or "wait." I will wait on You, Lord.*

DAY 3

THE LORD IS MY SAVIOR

The LORD *is my rock and my fortress and my deliverer, my God, my rock, in whom I take refuge, my shield, and the horn of my salvation, my stronghold and my refuge, my savior; you save me from violence.* (2 Samuel 22:2–3)

Read: 2 Samuel 22:1–7

Do you ever feel as though you are constantly battling to survive? Maybe life seems like a series of unfortunate mishaps that never seem to end. David must have felt that way too. Yet he knew God as his Savior in times of trouble.

During his forty years as king, David wrote much of the book of Psalms, a treasure trove of prayers and praises to our God. Though the Lord chose David to replace Saul as the king of Israel, the young man was not immediately seated on the throne. Instead, David first served Saul by playing the lyre to calm him. Next, David fought Goliath, claiming victory in the name of the Lord. (David's story is told in the books of Samuel; 1 Kings 1–2; and 1 Chronicles.)

In the midst of David's increasing success, there was trouble to come. Saul tried repeatedly to kill David, chasing him through the countryside. David lived with his men in caves, fighting and deceiving other enemies from foreign nations. Still, Saul chased David. Then David's family was captured by the Amalekites, and he fought to rescue them. When Saul finally died, David's rule over Israel was still not without trials. There was betrayal and battle, death and victory. There was even trouble in David's family. His son Ammon raped his daughter

Tamar, and his son Absalom murdered Ammon, then betrayed David. Again, David and his followers were chased through the countryside, this time by Absalom and his allies.

After the Lord delivered David from his enemies, the king penned his prayer in 2 Samuel 22. Throughout his struggles, David never lost sight of the fact that God and God alone was his Savior. In fact, even as he ran through the countryside, avoiding certain death, David trusted the Lord's plan for him.

David writes about God's salvation in his prayer in 2 Samuel 22:26–28 (NLT):

> *To the faithful you show yourself faithful; to those with integrity you show integrity. To the pure you show yourself pure, but to the crooked you show yourself shrewd. You rescue the humble, but your eyes watch the proud and humiliate them.*

You probably don't have anyone throwing spears at your head today. Yet the Lord is your Savior in your day-to-day struggles, providing your daily bread. After all, everything we have is from God. For all who believe in Jesus and repent of their sin, God is our Savior in eternity as well. Not one of us can be found faithful, blameless, or pure without the forgiveness of Christ. When we turn to Jesus, though, we are saved.

Pray: *Lord, I praise You for being my rock, my fortress, and my deliverer. When times are hard, I run to You for refuge. You are my Savior—not just from the hardships of this world, but from my sins too. You make me faithful, blameless, and pure, and it is You alone who are worthy to be praised.*

DAY 4

YOURS IS THE KINGDOM, O LORD

> *Yours, O Lord, is the greatness and the power and the glory and the victory and the majesty, for all that is in the heavens and in the earth is yours. Yours is the kingdom, O Lord, and you are exalted as head above all.*
>
> (1 Chronicles 29:11)

Read: 1 Chronicles 29:10–19

Do you ever struggle to share with others? Have you considered that cheerful giving is an act of praise? Our God is generous with us when we come to Him with our needs.

King David organized the worship of God in Israel. He made sure the priests and musicians were well prepared for the work and duties of praising the Lord. God did not allow David, a warrior, to build a temple where His people could gather to worship Him, so David gathered the raw materials needed for the temple and directed Solomon to build it after his death. David called together the people of Israel and told them of the great riches he had assembled. There were piles of gold, silver, bronze, iron, wood, stones, and gems. David's worship through giving inspired the people to worship God also, and they brought additional offerings of precious metals and stones. Then, David praised the Lord before the assembly of God's people.

Do you recognize the phrase, "*Yours is the kingdom*"? Jesus echoes David's words in the last stanza of the Lord's Prayer in Matthew 6:9–13 (NKJV): "*For Yours is the kingdom and the power and the glory forever. Amen.*" God's kingdom consists of every believer from all nations and people groups throughout history. One day, we will gather together to praise God, not at a temple made of gold and gemstones, but in the New Jerusalem, where we will praise Jesus forever. (See Revelation 21:22–23.)

Until we join the Lord in eternity, we praise Him with our words. Like the people of Israel, we also praise God with our belongings, our talents, and our time. David prayed, "*But who am I, and what is my people, that we should be able thus to offer willingly? For all things come from you, and of your own have we given you*" (1 Chronicles 29:14). Paul echoes this thought in 2 Corinthians 9:7 when he writes, "*God loves a cheerful giver.*" He adds, "*And God is able to make all grace abound to you, so that having all sufficiency in all things at all times, you may abound in every good work*" (verse 8).

Prayerful giving is an act of praise. We are able to give because our generous God first gives to us. As you cheerfully give to others in the name of Jesus, you do valuable work for the kingdom of God—the assembly of all believers who are ruled by our great king, Jesus.

Pray: *Lord, You are the Father of all who love You for eternity. All greatness, power, glory, victory, and majesty belong to You. Help me remember that all things come from You. When I give to You, I am giving from Your hand. Help me to recognize the abundance You have given to me, so that I may give to others in Your name. I want to praise You by being a cheerful giver, focused on Your kingdom.*

DAY 5
HOW MAJESTIC IS YOUR NAME

O Lord, our Lord, how majestic is your name in all the earth! You have set your glory above the heavens.

(Psalm 8:1)

Read: Psalm 8

Have you ever looked up at the stars on a clear, dark night? Though we can see only a small part of the cosmos from our backyards, the universe is immense. Our sun is just one of roughly one hundred to four hundred billion stars in the Milky Way Galaxy. Amazingly, the Milky Way is just one of thousands—maybe tens of thousands or even millions—of galaxies in the universe. We can only guess how many galaxies there truly are, as scientists continue to discover more. We humans are very small indeed.

Consider the magnificent God who created a galaxy large enough to contain billions of stars, then created galaxy after galaxy next to each other, each filled with stars and planets. Then, within our own massive galaxy, He created a perfectly spaced spinning rotation of planets and moons around the sun. God made a world exactly the right distance from the sun so that we could live on a beautiful globe, surrounded by thundering waterfalls, towering mountains, and peaceful plains.

God filled our world with weird and spectacular creatures and then set us here to worship Him. It is easy to imagine that the God of the universe would be disinterested in our short lives. But take a moment to ponder what David writes:

> *When I look at your heavens, the work of your fingers, the moon and the stars, which you have set in place, what is man that you are mindful of him, and the son of man that you care for him? Yet you have made him a little lower than the heavenly beings and crowned him with glory and honor.* (Psalm 8:3–5)

Jesus told us, *"Indeed, the very hairs of your head are all numbered"* (Luke 12:7 NIV). It is nearly unfathomable that the God who set the events of history on the timeline He created also knows the number of hairs on your head at this precise moment, isn't it? Yet, God cares for each moment of your life because He cares for you.

The acronym ACTS is often used as a guide for structuring prayer. When we pray, we first *adore* God. We *confess* our sins to our Savior. We *thank* Him for the great things He has done. Last, we humbly bring our requests before God in *supplication*. When we remember that we are praying to the God whose name is magnificent throughout the earth and who has covered the earth with His majesty, it is with great joy that we can praise the God who knows every star and planet as well as our every worry and concern.

Pray: *O Lord, You alone are the one who put the moon and the stars in their place. You made each creature creatively unique. You also created humans, and You care enough about our lives to allow the young and weak to uncover your magnificence as the strong who oppose You are silenced. May I always praise Your holy name.*

DAY 6

JESUS NEVER CHANGES

But you remain the same, and your years will never end.
(Hebrews 1:12 NIV)

Read: Hebrews 1:1–12

Have you ever been in an unsteady relationship? Perhaps you had no idea what would occur from one day to the next. Imagine how unsettling our lives would be if our Lord Jesus Christ changed. Yet we can rely on Him to never change.

In the first chapter of Hebrews, the curtain is pulled back on the throne room of God, and we witness God the Father address both angels and God the Son. First, we learn through His prophets that God promised the coming of His Son, Jesus, on Earth. Scripture affirms the miraculous birth of Jesus, and that He is truly God and truly man, so He could take the punishment for the sins of those who believe in Him. He was crucified, purifying us from sin. Then God the Father raised Jesus, God the Son, from the dead. Jesus ascended to heaven, and one day, He will return to call all who believe in Him and repent of their sins to eternal life. Those who rebel against God will be judged by Jesus.

Our salvation is amazing. Yet it is just a part of what we learn about our Lord Jesus in the first chapter of Hebrews. We also learn that Jesus is God. God the Father created the world through God the Son, and Jesus upholds the universe by the word of His power. Today, the risen Christ sits at the right hand of the Father.

We also learn that Jesus is above the angels, for He is their Creator. In fact, the angels worship Jesus. If the angels worship Jesus, how much more ought we bow to our knee before our Savior and Creator in prayer?

Next, God the Father announces that Jesus's throne over His kingdom will last forever, and He will rule with justice and in joy. Jesus loves righteousness and hates wickedness. One day, the heavens and Earth will wear out, just like your favorite sweater. Then, Jesus will switch everything out for a new, flawless heaven and earth that will be untarnished by human rebellion. The apostle John recorded part of his vision in Revelation 21:1 (NIV), writing, "*Then I saw 'a new heaven and a new earth,' for the first heaven and the first earth had passed away, and there was no longer any sea.*"

We will live with Jesus forever, and He promises us that He will be the same in eternity as He is today. For He tells us, "*Jesus Christ is the same yesterday and today and forever*" (Hebrews 13:8 NIV). What a blessing it is to know that our great Savior, God the Son, Jesus Christ our Lord, never changes. In fact, you can count on that.

Pray: *Lord Jesus Christ, You are the same yesterday, today, and forever. I praise You as the Creator of the universe. Thank You for holding all things together by Your powerful word. You have given me eternal life and purified me, erasing the record of my sin. Even the angels adore You. Help me to worship You always.*

DAY 7

WORTHY IS THE LAMB

And they sang a new song with these words: "You are worthy to take the scroll and break its seals and open it. For you were slaughtered, and your blood has ransomed people for God from every tribe and language and people and nation." (Revelation 5:9 NLT)

Read: Revelation 5:6–14

Have you considered what it would have been like to live in Old Testament times when the Israelites used a portable sanctuary called a tabernacle? The yearly Passover festival was a celebration of the fact that though each person's sin made them unworthy, God allowed a substitute—a perfect, worthy lamb—to pay the price for their sin. Jesus, our Lamb, is worthy of all our praise.

Had you lived during those ancient days, your yearly sacrifice of a Passover lamb would have been a sad reminder that your rebellion against God is worthy of death. After the lamb was slain, a priest would have mixed coals from the altar of sacrifice in a censer with a precious incense to be offered in the holy place. Your sins were forgiven through the sacrifice of the lamb, and your prayers were offered as a sweet incense to God.

In chapter 5 of John's revelation, we see the risen, slain Lamb of God, Jesus, standing in the throne room, where there are prayers and hymns of praise. Today, there is no need for an altar of sacrifice in the heavenly royal place. That is because Jesus's sacrifice has paid the price for the sins of believers *"once for all"* (Hebrews 10:10).

Just as the golden altar of incense in the tabernacle symbolized bringing the sweet smell of the saints' prayers before God, the prayers of the saints are shown being presented to the Lamb in heaven in golden bowls of incense. What a beautiful image. Both the Old Testament tabernacle and the New Testament throne room show our prayers as a pleasant aroma to our Lord and Savior.

In the throne room, the four living creatures that attend to Jesus and the twenty-four elders—the heads of the twelve tribes of Israel along with the twelve apostles—fall down before the Lamb, singing that He is worthy. Millions of angels sing there as well. By the blood of Jesus, God has saved people from every tribe, language, and nation to rule together with Him on the new earth. One day, every creature in heaven and on earth, under the earth and in the sea, will sing that all blessing, honor, glory, and power belong to the Lamb. What a joyous scene!

Maybe the circumstances of your life seem overwhelming at times. On the sleepless nights when you worry, struggle to envision the future, or miss the people you've lost, remember the throne room where your prayers are carried in golden bowls before the King of everything. Jesus is worthy of your praise, and He cares for your concerns.

Pray: *Jesus, You alone are worthy of my praise. One day, I will stand before You with the citizens of Your kingdom—all believers from every tribe, language, and nation throughout time. I will praise You with millions of angels and the heroes of Scripture. Until that day, my prayers are a sweet incense in Your throne room. Praise Your name.*

DAY 8
YOU ALONE ARE HOLY

Who will not fear, O Lord, and glorify your name? For you alone are holy. All nations will come and worship you, for your righteous acts have been revealed. (Revelation 15:4)

Read: Revelation 15:2–4

Have you ever earnestly prayed for justice? Perhaps you asked God for the successful investigation of a crime against a loved one, or for truth to prevail during a custody hearing for children you care about. Maybe you petitioned God in anguish over the morning news.

Our God is a God of grace—He forgives the crimes of those who believe in Him and repent. That is a blessing beyond measure. Our God is also a God of justice. He is a good Judge, and He has promised to bring complete justice in the end. That is because God is holy—He is perfect, pure, and without sin.

Back in the throne room of God, as the time approaches when God will make all things right and bring a final just ruling in heaven and on earth, those waiting and praying for justice begin to rejoice. It is a marvelous vision that John has: all who have conquered Satan and who serve the Lord stand with harps of God on a sea of glass mingled with fire, while angels wait to serve the final judgment of the just King. This gathering of the people of God sings the song of Moses and the song of the Lamb.

Singing praise to God over the end of the earth may seem a bit garish, but remember your sincere, painful prayers for justice. One day, God will bring a final justice when Jesus returns for His people. It will be an event filled with joy as the sinful, broken earth is ended, and those who hate God and His people are sentenced.

Then God will create a new heaven and a new earth for us to live on with Him. At the end of the trial of mankind, God announces the beginning of eternity:

> *Then He who sat on the throne said, "Behold, I make all things new." And He said to me, "Write, for these words are true and faithful." (Revelation 21:5* NKJV*)*

Imagine a world where there is no pain or brokenness. Every inhabitant will worship God as righteous and true and holy. Every nation will bow before Him. There will be no crime, no homelessness, no illness, and no hateful acts. It is no wonder that the throne room of heaven bursts into song at the promise of Jesus bringing the coming of eternity.

Pray: *Lord, You have done many wonderful things, both in Scripture and in the world around me. I have seen You act in my own life for my good. You are the King of nations, the true and just Judge. I know that one day all knees will bow before You in worship. Then everything You have done will be revealed. Until then, I trust Your holy name. You will bring justice for all wrong, whether it is now or in just a little while. Help me to be patient as I wait for You.*

PRAYERS OF THANKSGIVING

Give thanks in all circumstances; for this is the will of God in Christ Jesus for you.
—1 Thessalonians 5:18

We thank God for all He has done.

DAY 9

GOD MADE ME LAUGH

And Sarah said, "God has made me laugh, and all who hear will laugh with me." (Genesis 21:6 NKJV)

Read: Genesis 21:1–7

How many ways have you laughed? We laugh when we are amused, surprised, or even delighted. We can also laugh mockingly or contemptuously. Sarah laughed first in disbelief at the Lord's promise to her, then in thankful joy. Like Sarah, our faith is in our God who keeps His promises. Our faith cannot be in our own ability to have faith.

God said to Sarah's husband, Abraham, *"Look now toward heaven, and count the stars if you are able to number them. ... So shall your descendants be"* (Genesis 15:5 NKJV). From Abraham's promised heirs, God would build the nation of Israel.

When God first promised Abraham a son through Sarah, she was in her sixties, and Abraham was seventy-five. Sarah didn't trust God to keep His promise without her intervention, so she instituted the ultimate work-around by handing her Egyptian servant, Hagar, over to Abraham as a second wife. As a result, Hagar had a son, Ishmael, with Abraham.

Yet God restated His promise to give Abraham and Sarah a son several times. When the Lord and two angels visited Abraham, Sarah listened at the door of the tent while the Lord promised that when He returned in a year, Sarah would be holding a son. Was Sarah overjoyed? No. In fact, Sarah was way past childbearing age and could not see how God would—or maybe could—keep His promise to her. So she laughed in derision and unbelief.

> *The* Lord *said to Abraham, "Why did Sarah laugh and say, 'Shall I indeed bear a child, now that I am old?' Is anything too hard for the* Lord*? At the appointed time I will return to you, about this time next year, and Sarah shall have a son." But Sarah denied it, saying, "I did not laugh," for she was afraid. He said, "No, but you did laugh."*
>
> (Genesis 18:13–15)

Scripture doesn't tell us about Sarah's prayers during that year of waiting on God's promise. But Hebrews 11:11 (NKJV) says, *"By faith Sarah herself also received strength to conceive seed, and she bore a child when she was past the age, because she judged Him faithful who had promised."* Sarah believed our faithful God and His word, and twenty-five years after His initial promise to give her a son with Abraham, ninety-year-old Sarah held her baby Isaac in her arms. Rather than laugh in derision, she laughed in pure joy.

When you encounter a promise from God in His Word, you can thank Him in joy. Even if the fulfillment of God's promise seems far off, have faith that His Word is true. When you read that God tells us that He hears our prayers, know that He does. You can thank God for His promises that Jesus is returning, that He forgets the sins of believers, and that one day, everyone who is saved will live with Jesus for eternity.

Pray: *Lord, I thank You that Your Word is true and praise You for being faithful. I know I can trust Your promises to me for forgiveness, salvation, provision, and care. Help me to live in joyful laughter over Your goodness.*

DAY 10

THE LORD HAS TRIUMPHED

And Miriam sang this song: "Sing to the Lord, for he has triumphed gloriously; he has hurled both horse and rider into the sea." (Exodus 15:21 NLT)

Read: Exodus 15:19–21

Have you ever found yourself in an absolutely impossible situation with no apparent way out? Insurmountable problems often move us to pray. Sometimes we don't hit our knees until the moment we realize there is no other route of escape. That is when we remember that God is our rescuer.

When God sent Moses and his brother Aaron to lead the Israelites out of enslavement to the most powerful nation on earth, He led them right into an impossible situation on purpose, stranding them by design. He said to Moses:

> *And I will harden the hearts of the Egyptians, and they will charge in after the Israelites. My great glory will be displayed through Pharaoh and his troops, his chariots, and his charioteers. When my glory is displayed through them, all Egypt will see my glory and know that I am the Lord!*
> (Exodus 14:17–18 NLT)

Camped on the edge of the Red Sea, the Israelite families watched as Pharaoh and his entire Egyptian army barreled down on them. However, the Israelites did not pray; instead they wailed and moaned. "Did Egypt not have enough graves? Is that why you brought us to die in the wilderness?" they asked Moses. (See Exodus 14:11.)

But God was glorified when He parted the Red Sea so His people could flee to the other side on dry land, then collapsed the waters on the entire Egyptian army. It is easy to imagine the Sinai wilderness as a barren place without cities or encampments, since the people of Israel avoided them. The reality is there were many people living in that wilderness, and all of them likely heard how God rescued His people.

It was after this spectacular deliverance that Moses and Aaron's sister, Miriam, led the women of Israel in a public and joyful prayer to the Lord. With tambourines and dancing, the women sang to God. We might wrinkle our noses today at God's violent rescue of the Israelites. But we must remember that the Israelite women were joyfully thanking God for saving their babies and children, mothers and fathers, husbands and friends from a savage, angry army.

Scripture tells us that Miriam and her brothers walked out of Egypt at the head of a caravan of over six hundred thousand men, along with their wives and children. (See Numbers 1:44–46.) Imagine the joyful noise that roughly six hundred thousand women made as they thanked the Lord with all their might. What glory that brought to God, our Rescuer.

When life is hard, you can thank God that He hears your prayers. He is ready and able to save you. When your circumstances seem utterly hopeless, thank God that He is the God who rescues.

Pray: *Lord, I believe You saved the Israelites, throwing the horses and riders into the sea. I see how You are answering my prayers today. Let me remember to thank You, loudly and with joy. Let me too remember to give thanks to You with my sisters in Christ, so our joyful noise will bring glory to Your name as our neighbors see Your work in our lives.*

DAY 11
YOU SEARCH ME AND KNOW ME

Search me, God, and know my heart; test me and know my anxious thoughts. See if there is any offensive way in me, and lead me in the way everlasting.

(Psalm 139:23–24 NIV)

Read: Psalm 139

Have you ever woken up out of a sound sleep, suddenly remembering a moment when you felt overexposed? Perhaps you worry that people will discover something true about you or your past, and you struggle to let go of it. Maybe you fear something about your health, your personality, or your abilities is less than adequate for the life you're living. No matter what others think, God already knows everything about you.

When David wrote Psalm 139 as a song of thankfulness to be used by God's people in worship, he likely knew the fear of exposure. After all, David certainly had his share of cringe-worthy moments. He was a sinner and probably not up to the task of leading God's people. Yet David knew the God who knows us.

Like the men and women of Israel who sang David's song of thanks to God for His intimate knowledge of their lives, you can also rest in the knowledge that God searches and knows you. In fact, He specifically formed you. Our great, loving God sees all your actions—even those as trivial as going to bed and rising for the day. God knows each of your thoughts, and He knows how you respond to day-to-day triumphs and struggles. God even knows your words before you speak them.

God formed you in the womb and was involved in shaping every aspect of who you are. He knows your thoughts, the things that stress you, and even your sins. As Christians, we can thank our amazing God that He searches and knows us. The Lord of heaven and earth does not seek to condemn His forgiven saints. Rather, He guides, directs, and comforts them.

God surrounds you, He lays His hand on you, and He leads you in the eternal way of His truth. There is nowhere you can go where you will be lost from His love or from His care. God even protects you from the wicked who wish you harm, just because you belong to Him.

What a blessing it is to understand that the Creator of all things knows every single thing about each of us. He walks through life with us, His precious creations. When believers stand before Christ on the final day, there will be no accusation that will overcome Christ's love. You can sleep well, knowing you are known and cared for.

Pray: *Heavenly Father, thank You for forming me in my mother's womb, making my frame and my soul. Thank You that every one of my days has already been formed for me by You and has been written in Your book. I am so grateful that there is nowhere I can go where You will lose track of me. You protect me and lead me, helping me to become more and more like Jesus. You even see the things in me that grieve You, yet You do not turn away.*

DAY 12
YOU HAVE DONE WONDERFUL THINGS

Lord, you are my God; I will exalt you and praise your name, for in perfect faithfulness you have done wonderful things, things planned long ago. (Isaiah 25:1 NIV)

Read: Isaiah 25:1–9

Do you keep a daily gratitude journal, recording what God has done for you? Throughout Scripture, God instituted memorials and feasts to help us remember His faithfulness. Maybe that is because we have short memories or tend to focus on the negative things in life. Whatever the reason, God's Word reminds us to remember the great things God has done, looking forward to what He will do in the future.

In Isaiah chapters 24 through 27, the prophet focuses on the time in history when God will bring an end to all oppression, all war, and all wickedness. God's people will no longer fear tyrannical leaders, foreign invaders, or ruthless hackers. We won't need walled cities, strong armies, or smart technology to protect us because God will remove evil from our lives altogether. He alone will be our protector.

We can imagine that the saints in heaven sing a prayer to the Lord our God with the words of Isaiah 25. It is a strange truth that we are living in the time of "already but not yet." God has already executed His great plan for our salvation through Jesus. Jesus has already paid the price for the sins of all who believe in Him. Death is already conquered. But we have not yet seen the end of the story. Evil has not yet been eradicated from this world. We are not yet living forever on the new earth in our glorified bodies, and we have not yet seen the end of all death.

One day, though, the commander of heaven's armies will gather together all those who love Jesus. Believers from every nation throughout time will feast together as they celebrate that death is no more. John tells us about Jesus's coming new heaven and new earth:

> *He will wipe every tear from their eyes. There will be no more death" or mourning or crying or pain, for the old order of things has passed away.* (Revelation 21:4 NIV)

Jesus has already conquered death and grief, and one day, we will see victory in full. It can be difficult to focus on eternity, which has not yet arrived. But we can easily thank God for the great things He has already done in our lives up to this point. Just as He planned those acts for our benefit, He will one day bring us to the marvelous place where He will wipe every tear away.

Pray: *Lord, You have done wonderful things in Scripture, in history, and in my life. I know You planned all these events long ago, and nothing is a surprise to You. Thank You for all You have given me and how You care for me each day. Help me to remember that when I believe in Jesus and turn from my sins, I already have a place at the feast where You will wipe away my tears.*

DAY 13

HIS MERCY IS FOR THOSE WHO FEAR HIM

And his mercy is for those who fear him from generation to generation. (Luke 1:50)

Read: Luke 1:46–55

Do you celebrate Christ's birth by giving gifts to those who contribute to your life in some way? Perhaps you also set aside a gift for someone in need as an act of mercy. God's mercy is His gift to believers of kindness, love, and compassion. We do not deserve God's mercy, and we cannot earn it. Instead, salvation in Jesus is a totally undeserved, unearned mercy on us. It is the greatest gift we can ever receive.

When Mary prayed to God, she thanked Him for His mercy. She knew exactly how wonderful Jesus's gift to the world would be. Shortly before her song of praise, Mary received a visit from the angel Gabriel. He told Mary she would have a miraculous, virgin pregnancy and birth through the power of the Holy Spirit.

Gabriel also told Mary about the baby she was to carry:

And behold, you will conceive in your womb and bear a son, and you shall call his name Jesus. He will be great and will be called the Son of the Most High. And the Lord God will give to him the throne of his father David, and he will reign over the house of Jacob forever, and of his kingdom there will be no end. (Luke 1:31–33)

What an amazing promise Mary received! She would bear the Son of God, who would sit on the throne of the kingdom of heaven.

Mary's prayer, often called the Magnificat, is one of the best-known prayers in Scripture. She is, after all, thanking God for the coming salvation of all who believe in Jesus. As in many of the thanksgiving psalms, Mary praises God. Then, she expresses her gratitude specifically for what God has done and what He is doing.

Mary thanks God for His mercy on all who honor and respect Him throughout the generations. God's salvation and gift of eternal life is for anyone who turns from sin and follows Jesus as their Lord and Savior. She thanks God for judging the proud of heart, the mighty rulers, the rich and the greedy. God seeks out those who are humble and in need, and He blesses them with salvation and with provision for their daily needs. The promise of eternal life with Jesus stretches throughout the Bible, from Genesis to Revelation.

Mary thanks God for His wonderful gift of the Savior, Jesus Christ. Our rebellion against God has separated us from Him. But God loves us so much that He sent Jesus, God the Son, to be born both fully God and fully human, to live a sinless life, and to take the punishment for our sins upon Himself. It is the reason Jesus was crucified and died. Three days later, He was raised from the dead. Jesus ascended to heaven to the Father, but one day, He will return to gather believers to eternal life with Him.

Pray: *Father, I know I have rebelled against You. I thank You for sending Jesus, my Savior, to forgive my sins forever. Thank You for Your great mercy on all believers. Your gift to us through Your Son is unmerited and unearned. Help me to fear You, to honor and respect You.*

DAY 14

HE MADE US A FAMILY

I thank my God in all my remembrance of you.

(Philippians 1:3)

Read: Philippians 1:3–11

Have you gathered with another group of believers on a regular basis? Maybe you meet weekly for a Bible study, you visit for a potluck meal, or you gather for a monthly outing. Have you ever noticed that as you pray for other believers, you have them in your heart? That is because God makes us a family. As we pray for and with other believers in Christ, a special bond forms. When we meet to do gospel work, God knits us together in unity. We begin to love and enjoy those who also love Jesus.

When he wrote his letter to the Philippians, Paul was in prison. We might expect his opening greeting to be a request for prayer for his own freedom or endurance. Instead, Paul told the people of Philippi he was thanking God for them and praying with joy because of their work in the gospel. In fact, Acts 16 tells us that Paul, Silas, and Timothy met their new friend Lydia in Philippi when they visited a place of prayer at the riverbank. After the men shared the gospel with the women praying there, Lydia came to faith in Jesus.

As the men continued to share the gospel at the place of prayer, a possessed, fortune-telling girl followed them day after day. She informed everyone that Paul and Silas were "*servants of the Most High God, who proclaim to you the way of salvation*" (Acts 16:17). When Paul commanded the evil spirit to leave her, he and Silas were dragged to the marketplace, attacked, stripped and beaten with rods, then jailed in stocks.

God responded to Paul and Silas's prayers by sending an earthquake to open the doors of the prison. Rather than leave the prison, Paul shared the gospel with the jailer. Then he, his wife, and his entire family were saved.

The Philippian church was grounded in prayer. We can be certain that as Paul wrote his letter, he was remembering Lydia, the demon-freed girl, the jailer and his wife, and the Jewish women who gathered at the place of prayer. Paul remembered his friends with joy, knowing that Jesus was still working in their lives. He prayed for their love to overflow and for their knowledge and discernment to grow as well. Praying for them brought him joy and assurance that they would continue to grow in Christ.

Do you have a place of prayer, like the women of Philippi, where you gather with other believers to come before God? Have you developed a regular habit of praying for other Christians as you remember them? This week, take some time to consider how you can grow in your prayer life for and with your family in Christ.

Pray: *Jesus, thank You for my sisters and brothers in Christ. Their membership in the family of grace is such a blessing to me. I ask that You would complete the good work You have started in them. Help them to grow in love, in their knowledge of Scripture, and in godly wisdom. Let their lives be lived for the glory of God. Thank You for this wonderful family You have placed me in.*

DAY 15

BORN AGAIN TO A LIVING HOPE

> *Blessed be the God and Father of our Lord Jesus Christ! According to his great mercy, he has caused us to be born again to a living hope through the resurrection of Jesus Christ from the dead.* (1 Peter 1:3)

Read: 1 Peter 1:3–5

Have you ever been promised something you really hoped would happen? Maybe it was a trip, a gift, or a relationship. Sometimes, promises made by people are not kept. We can rest assured, though, that our good, honest, and sovereign God will keep all of His promises. In fact, God is the promise—He is our inheritance.

In the Bible, the word *hope* means something different than it does in our everyday use of the word. We do not just desire good things from God, wishing they would come true. Instead, because God is trustworthy, we expectantly wait for our God to do everything He has said He will do. We serve a God who keeps His promises.

Peter learned that lesson over time. Jesus clearly told Peter and the disciples that He would rise from the dead.

> *And he began to teach them that the Son of Man must suffer many things and be rejected by the elders and the chief priests and the scribes and be killed, and after three days rise again.* (Mark 8:31)

Peter confessed his belief in Jesus, stating, *"You are the Christ, the Son of the living God"* (Matthew 16:16). He knew Jesus is the Messiah promised by God, the one who was sent to take away the sins of the world. Yet when Jesus was arrested, Peter publicly denied knowing Him. In fact, Peter watched Jesus's crucifixion from a distance. (See Luke 23:49.) When Mary Magdalene returned from the empty tomb to tell Peter and John that Jesus's body was gone, Peter raced John to site of the resurrection. There, he found that Jesus was, in fact, raised from the dead. Later, Jesus appeared to Peter—resurrected and alive for eternity. (See John 20:1–23.)

In his first letter, when Peter writes his blessing on *"the God and Father of our Lord Jesus Christ,"* he includes the readers of his letter in his prayer. We can be unendingly thankful because God had mercy on us. Believers are born again—saved—into a living hope because Jesus died for our sins.

We do not hope without basis that we will be raised again. Instead, we know that Jesus paid the price for our sins, then He rose from the dead. He is in heaven, guarding our inheritance. If we believe in Jesus, we too will be resurrected to glorified bodies. We do not even have to hope that our belief will be strong enough. Instead, we are protected by God's power.

Your faith in Jesus and His saving grace, along with your repentance, is enough.

Pray: *Lord, You truly are the God and Father of my Lord Jesus Christ, and I thank You for Your great mercy. I am expectantly waiting for You to fulfill the promise You made me of welcoming me into Your kingdom and adopting me as Your child. My inheritance in You is incorruptible, undefiled, and unfading. Praise Your name!*

PRAYERS OF CONFESSION

If we confess our sins, he is faithful and just to forgive us our sins and to cleanse us from all unrighteousness.
—1 John 1:9

We admit our sin to the God who saves us.

DAY 16

WE HAVE SINNED AGAINST GOD

Finally, they cried out to the Lord *for help, saying, "We have sinned against you because we have abandoned you as our God and have served the images of Baal."*

(Judges 10:10 NLT)

Read: Judges 10:6–16

Have you ever noticed that some cycles in life seem difficult to change? For instance, if you habitually forget to move your wet laundry from the washer to the dryer, you may have to wash each load twice because it's become musty. Breaking a cycle of sin—like cursing God's name or gossiping about others—is a much bigger deal. We can take comfort that our righteousness doesn't come from within ourselves, nor can we earn righteousness. Rather, God credits believers with Jesus's righteousness.

In the days discussed in the book of Judges, the Israelites struggled to overcome a destructive cycle of apostasy. The people would worship idols, then God would discipline them by allowing other nations to conquer them. When the people were in enough pain, they would cry out to God, repenting of their sin, and God would send a judge to rescue them. Then after a period of peace, the people would worship idols again.

After seven judges and seven cycles of apostasy then a return to peace, the people of Israel abandoned the Lord, bowing to fake gods made with human hands once again. So God allowed them to be oppressed by the Ammonites. After nearly two decades of suffering under the Ammonites, the Israelites finally confessed their rebellion against their Creator.

> *Did I not rescue you from the Egyptians, the Amorites, the Ammonites, the Philistines, the Sidonians, the Amalekites, and the Maonites? When they oppressed you, you cried out to me for help, and I rescued you. Yet you have abandoned me and served other gods. So I will not rescue you anymore. Go and cry out to the gods you have chosen! Let them rescue you in your hour of distress!* (Judges 10:11–14 NLT)

God would no longer rescue His people. Instead, they could turn for help to the wooden, stone, and metal idols they loved. That's when the people finally put away their "gods." Again, they asked their Creator God for help, confessing, *"We have sinned"* (Judges 10:15). Our God, who is ever merciful and righteous, rescued them once again.

Today, the idea of idolatry seems strange. Most of us do not bow to statues, yet idolatry is the worship of anything we put ahead of our Father God. If you find yourself giving your thoughts, your time, or your money to something in particular, it is a good idea to ask whether you are honoring God or rebelling in your heart. Are you faithfully worshipping your Savior and glorifying your God, praying in the Spirit and remaining in the Word?

If breaking a sin cycle in your life is a challenge, you can ask God for help. God is our righteousness. We do not need to rely on our own ability to be good.

Pray: *Jesus, you taught us,* "Seek the Kingdom of God above all else, and live righteously, and he will give you everything you need" *(Matthew 6:33 NLT). I see the areas of my life where I am repeating sinful behavior. I have sinned against You. Please help me seek You and Your kingdom. Please give me Your righteousness.*

DAY 17
TAKE AWAY MY INIQUITY

And David's heart condemned him after he had numbered the people. So David said to the Lord, "I have sinned greatly in what I have done; but now, I pray, O Lord, take away the iniquity of Your servant, for I have done very foolishly."
(2 Samuel 24:10 NKJV)

Read: 2 Samuel 24:10–17

Pride is a sneaky sin, isn't it? There is nothing wrong with doing our best work when it brings glory to God. In fact, Paul tells us to do just that: "*And whatever you do, do it heartily, as to the Lord and not to men, knowing that from the Lord you will receive the reward of the inheritance; for you serve the Lord Christ*" (Colossians 3:23–24 NKJV). Problems arise when we begin to feel entirely self-sufficient, or when we work for our own glory rather than for God's. For God will be glorified.

Nearing the end of his life, David decided to count the number of fighting-aged men under his command. Scripture tells us that Satan "*incited David to number Israel*" (1 Chronicles 21:1) and God "*incited David*" to do so (2 Samuel 24:1). It seems that God allowed Satan to tempt David. In turn, David failed the test of his faith, turning from his trust in God toward self-reliance. So David pridefully took stock of his army. Nearly ten months later, when the census was complete, David confessed his foolish sin, asking God to remove his iniquity.

Iniquity isn't a word we use often. Put simply, iniquity is sin we plan to commit. It is premeditated and habitual self-glorification that we allow to become a regular part of our lives. All sin separates us from God. To become children of God, we must believe in Jesus and turn from our sin. Iniquity is the exact opposite of turning from sin toward Jesus.

When David petitioned God to remove his iniquity, he was asking God to excise the sin that was rooted in his heart, producing rotten fruit. People around David could see the rotten fruit, but only God could see the root of David's sin. In His mercy, God saves us from our sins.

Sin, though, carries consequences. In David's case, his pride cost seventy thousand men. (See 2 Samuel 24:15.) Yet, as God does, He brought beauty from the ashes, for the land David purchased to build an altar to the Lord was the same place David's son Solomon later built God's temple, where the people worshipped the Lord.

It is not easy to consider the habitual sin in our lives, particularly pride. Maybe that is because pride can disguise itself as conscientiousness, achievement, selflessness, and a myriad of other traits that are praised in our culture. The good news is that we can confess our self-glorification to God and ask Him to remove it. In His great mercy, God is faithful to help us.

Pray: *Lord, please remove the pride in my heart. Let me not work out of my own selfish ambition. Instead, let me work heartily for Your glory. Help me to have a heart of joyful service for You. Lord, help me to humbly remember I serve Your glory and not my own reputation.*

DAY 18
GREATLY HUMBLED

In his distress he sought the favor of the Lord *his God and humbled himself greatly before the God of his ancestors.*
(2 Chronicles 33:12 NIV)

Read: 2 Chronicles 33:1–20

Have you ever forgotten to secure the lid of your blender before turning it on? You probably ended up with goo all over your kitchen. The consequences of sin can be just like that—widely distributed and terribly messy. Sometimes God allows us to suffer the pain our sin causes so we will turn to Him in repentance. The blood of Jesus can cover any sin.

The far-flung consequences of King Manasseh of Judah's hideous, murderous rebellion against God led to a national tragedy. In 1 Corinthians 10:20, Paul tells us that sacrifices to idols are actually offered to demons. Not only did Manasseh build places for the people of Israel to worship demons, but he also sacrificed his sons to demons. Manasseh practiced the occult, visiting mediums and engaging in fortune-telling and sorcery. Today, we would call him a witch or a satanist.

Through His prophets, God called Manasseh and his people to repent. But they ignored God, continuing to seek out demons. So God brought a terrible judgment on Manasseh, and he was led away to Babylon with a hook in his nose and shackles on his wrists and ankles.

Despite all the terrible things Manasseh did, God responded to the exiled king's humble prayer of repentance by extending mercy and grace even to this terrible man who led his nation into the practice of the occult. Manasseh was forgiven, and he came to know the Lord as God. God restored Manasseh to his position as king in Jerusalem, where Manasseh put his new faith into action, pointing his subjects toward the rightful worship of God.

When we turn to God and ask for His mercy, He is faithful to forgive us. "*Godly sorrow brings repentance that leads to salvation and leaves no regret,*" says 2 Corinthians 7:10 (NIV). Sometimes, the Lord disciplines us here on earth so we will be humbled enough to seek Him. The pain of our circumstances today can save us an eternity of sorrow tomorrow. That is exactly what the Lord did for evil King Manasseh when He allowed him to be exiled.

If sin has created a widespread mess in your life, do not be discouraged. Now is the time to confess your sin to God and seek His mercy. After all, our great God "*is faithful and just to forgive*" (1 John 1:9).

There is more good news. If you have ever despaired of praying for those you know who seem beyond the reach of even God's hand, remember Manasseh. The wicked witch of a king sought the Lord, and God forgave him. Be faithful in prayer, waiting expectantly for the salvation of those you love.

Pray: *Lord, You are the God of those who have come before me, and You are my God too. Help me to humbly seek Your favor and to flee evil. Thank You for the story of Your love even for the evil King Manasseh. Help those I love to humble themselves and repent. Please bring them to faith in Jesus. Lord, extend Your mercy to my loved ones.*

DAY 19

YOU FORGAVE MY SIN

I acknowledged my sin to you, and I did not cover my iniquity; I said, "I will confess my transgressions to the Lord,*" and you forgave the iniquity of my sin.*

(Psalm 32:5)

Read: Psalm 32

Do you ever wonder why, if you are a new creature in Christ with a new heart, you still sin? It is a good question. Writing to fellow believers, John says, "*If we say we have no sin, we deceive ourselves, and the truth is not in us*" (1 John 1:8). We are saved, yet we struggle to do what is right. So John instructs us, "*If we confess our sins, he is faithful and just to forgive us our sins and to cleanse us from all unrighteousness*" (verse 9).

It is a wonderful truth that as soon as we believe in Jesus and repent of our sin, we are forgiven forever. We are in a relationship with God that will never end. Paul writes:

> *And you, who were dead in your trespasses and the uncircumcision of your flesh, God made alive together with him, having forgiven us all our trespasses, by canceling the record of debt that stood against us with its legal demands. This he set aside, nailing it to the cross.* (Colossians 2:13–14)

Our sin against God created a debt. When Jesus forgives us, that debt is canceled, nailed to the cross, where no one can attempt to make us pay for it. When we pray, we speak to God, who forgives all our sins.

Though we follow Christ, we still battle the temptations of this world and the deceit in our own hearts. The process of sanctification, of being made more like Jesus, is the work of the Holy Spirit in our lives. God involves us in our own sanctification. You become more like Jesus as you and the Holy Spirit work together.

In his prayer in Psalm 32, David's description of living with unconfessed sin is vivid. When we hide our sin from the Lord, we are like sick people. Our bones rot away, and we groan constantly. God, who knows exactly what we have thought and done, keeps His hand heavy on us as our strength withers. Yet when we finally break down and confess our failings to God, the relief and joy are enormous. God begins to teach and counsel us in the way we should go.

Psalm 32 concludes, "*Many are the sorrows of the wicked, but steadfast love surrounds the one who trusts in the* Lord. *Be glad in the* Lord, *and rejoice, O righteous, and shout for joy, all you upright in heart!*" (verses 10–11).

Pray: *My Lord, You are my delight and my salvation. I trust You, and I do not want to hide my sin from You. You know my heart and You see my thoughts. Let me acknowledge my sin and come to You for forgiveness. Please make my heart pure and clean before You. Help me to become more and more holy, like Jesus. Thank You for the joy of being upright in heart!*

DAY 20

CREATE IN ME A CLEAN HEART

Create in me a clean heart, O God, and renew a steadfast spirit within me. (Psalm 51:10 NKJV)

Read: Psalm 51

Are you ever overwhelmed by the reality that you are far from righteous? Do you battle with sloth, envy, greed, or anger? Our God creates a clean heart in us when we repent.

Paul struggled against sin too, writing, "*For the good that I will to do, I do not do; but the evil I will not to do, that I practice. Now if I do what I will not to do, it is no longer I who do it, but sin that dwells in me*" (Romans 7:19–20 NKJV). Like Paul, we often do the things we don't want to do, yet we don't do the things we know we should do.

David faced that same fight in 2 Samuel chapters 11 and 12. Walking on the roof of his palace, he saw Bathsheba bathing atop her house. When David called this married woman into a one-night affair, Bathsheba became pregnant. Rather than confessing the sexual sins of lust, covetousness, and adultery, David compounded his mess. First, he arranged for Bathsheba's soldier husband Uriah to visit his wife so he would assume the baby was his own. But Uriah refused to go home while his fellow soldiers were at battle, so David arranged for Uriah to die in action.

Still, Acts 13:22 (NKJV) quotes God as saying, "*I have found David the son of Jesse, a man after My own heart, who will do all My will.*" David cost Bathsheba both her husband and her firstborn son. He caused the death of Uriah and his fellow soldiers, robbing their families. Through his villainous deceit, David made Joab, the commander of his army, an accessory to murder. Yet God found David to be a man after His own heart. How could this be true?

David loved God, he desired to do God's will, and yet he struggled with his sin. After the prophet Nathan confronted David, David confessed his sin and repented. Paul describes this struggle in Romans 7:21–25 as a battle between our delight in God in our inner being and our flesh, which is captive to sin. It is Jesus Christ who delivers us from the fight.

Like David, you can cry out to God for mercy when you have fallen, asking Him to forgive your sins against Him. You can find delight in the Lord's truth and wisdom, asking Him to renew and cleanse your spirit and heart. God's salvation is a joy. He restores the joy, so you can teach others about God's ways. Our lives are the offering we bring to the Lord, and He is the one who gives us a new heart, making that offering possible.

Pray: *Father, sometimes it is easy for me to look around and feel good about the fact that I have not sinned as someone else has. Yet like Paul and like David, I often don't do what I want to do. I often do what I don't want to do. My flesh and my spirit are at war. Please create a clean heart in me. Forgive my sins, and help me to walk in righteousness, offering each day of my life to You.*

DAY 21

SALVATION BELONGS TO THE LORD

But I with the voice of thanksgiving will sacrifice to you; what I have vowed I will pay. Salvation belongs to the Lord!
(Jonah 2:9)

Read: Jonah 2

Have you ever found it difficult to pray for the salvation of those who oppose God? Perhaps, instead, it seems like some people do not even deserve God's grace. Yet our God saves whom He saves. In fact, salvation belongs to the Lord.

Jonah's job as a prophet was to call people to repentance wherever the Lord sent him. But when God called Jonah to go to Nineveh, the capital city of the evil and ruthless Assyrians, the prophet instead boarded a ship headed in the opposite direction. James 4:17 says, *"So whoever knows the right thing to do and fails to do it, for him it is sin."* It wasn't a sin, exactly, for Jonah to ride on a ship to Tarshish. Rather, his sin was that rather than obeying God, Jonah exalted his own feelings over God's will for him. He ran from God.

That was a bad idea. During a giant storm sent by God, Jonah told the terrified pagan sailors, *"I am a Hebrew, and I fear the Lord, the God of heaven, who made the sea and the dry land"* (Jonah 1:9). When their gods could not calm the storm, yet Jonah's God was in the control of the sea, those pagan sailors repented and were saved.

Jonah, though, was thrown overboard and swallowed by a giant fish. After three days and three nights, he was finally willing to confess his sin to God. Jonah gave thanks to God and acknowledged that salvation belongs to the Lord. It is God who saves, and He will have mercy on whom He will have mercy. (See Romans 9:15.)

After God had the fish vomit Jonah onto dry land so he could go to Nineveh, Jonah called the people to repent and follow God. The king of this great and terrible city not only repented, but he called everyone in the city—all one hundred twenty thousand people—to fast and repent. Even the cows were forced to fast, covered in sackcloth. God had mercy on the souls of the repentant people.

Everywhere Jonah went, God saved people. Jonah, though, was angry. He wanted to make his own decision to withhold salvation from those outside the people of God, the Israelites.

As Christians, we can fall into the trap of thinking we know who deserves God's mercy and love. We may even withhold the gospel from those we think are especially terrible. Yet God's salvation is His alone to give. The Lord has called us to love others and to share the good news of Jesus Christ with everyone. Is there someone heavy on your heart who needs to hear about the cross?

Pray: *Merciful God, I call out to You. You brought my life up from the pit, saving me. Forgive any hypocrisy or bias in me. Help me to give my life to You as I have vowed. Let me see the wicked as those who are in need of You. Salvation belongs to You, Lord. Thank You for saving me. Let me be an instrument of Your salvation in the lives of others.*

DAY 22
BE MERCIFUL TO ME

But the tax collector, standing far off, would not even lift up his eyes to heaven, but beat his breast, saying, "God, be merciful to me, a sinner!" (Luke 18:13)

Read: Luke 18:9–14

Have you ever witnessed a child make a demand laced with entitlement? It is unattractive to approach someone with an air of expectation or pride. Instead, our God answers our humble cries for mercy.

The Pharisee prayed, thanking God that he was not like other people. He wasn't a thief, unfair, or an adulterer. He also wasn't a tax collector who took money unjustly. In fact, the Pharisee told God, he followed rules perfectly, fasting twice a week and giving some money to God. Yet the man's prayer contained no adoration of God, nor any thanks for anything God had done in his life. There was no confession of sins. The Pharisee didn't ask God to grow his own character in the Spirit, nor to help anyone else. Instead, the man crowed about his goodness, then mocked the spiritual state of the tax collector.

How often are we tempted to act like the Pharisee, praying to God in willful expectation? We compare our sins to the sins of others and declare our rebellion acceptable. Paul writes, "*For by grace you have been saved through faith. And this is not your own doing; it is the gift of God, not a result of works, so that no one may boast*" (Ephesians 2:8–9). Not one of us is saved because of our own goodness or worthiness. Plain and simple, salvation is a gift.

In sharp contrast to the Pharisee, the tax collector came to God in sorrow over his sins. He identified himself as a sinner, and he humbly asked God for mercy. God is, indeed, merciful to the humble.

Our demeanor in prayer matters to God, just as the posture of our children matters when they approach us. As our good Father, God cares for us, and He wants to hear from us. He always answers our humble prayers.

In fact, Jesus was teaching about prayer when He said, *"Which of you fathers, if your son asks for a fish, will give him a snake instead? Or if he asks for an egg, will give him a scorpion? If you then, though you are evil, know how to give good gifts to your children, how much more will your Father in heaven give the Holy Spirit to those who ask him!"* (Luke 11:11–13 NIV).

As a Father, God's answers display His wisdom and His plan for this world and its people. Sometimes, He tells us *no* when we make a request. Yet when we come to Him humbly for the forgiveness of sin, His answer is always *yes*. What a good gift that truly is!

Pray: *God, be merciful to me, a sinner. Help me put away my pride, my greed, and my self-sufficiency. I rely on You for forgiveness of my sins, for my daily bread, for the strength to forgive others, and for the wisdom to flee temptation. Holy is Your name! May I remain humble before You.*

PRAYERS OF SUPPLICATION

Cast all your anxiety on him because he cares for you.
—1 Peter 5:7 (NIV)

We humbly ask God to provide for our needs.

DAY 23
THE GOD WHO SEES ME

Thereafter, Hagar used another name to refer to the Lord, who had spoken to her. She said, "You are the God who sees me." She also said, "Have I truly seen the One who sees me?" (Genesis 16:13 NLT)

Read: Genesis 16:1–16

Have you ever gone through a time so painful, you just didn't know how to pray? Perhaps you couldn't bring yourself to thank God for your circumstances or ask Him to do His will. In those times, it is a comfort to remember that God sees you.

Hagar must have felt unseen while serving Sarah in the land of Canaan. When Sarah grew impatient waiting for God's promise of a son, she gave her Egyptian servant, Hagar, to her husband, Abraham, as a surrogate. Once pregnant, Hagar felt her status should be that of a wife. This inflamed Sarah. So Abraham told Sarah to treat Hagar any way she wanted. Sarah made life so miserable for Hagar that the desperate woman ran away.

Hagar didn't flee into the wilderness so she would have a quiet place to address God. Yet God saw her distress and sent the angel of the Lord to speak to her. The angel asked Hagar what her plan was, then instructed her to do something entirely different. God blessed Hagar and her unborn son, Ishmael, promising to give Hagar more descendants than she could count. The angel of the Lord told Hagar, *"The Lord has heard your cry of distress"* (Genesis 16:11 NLT).

Hagar was still the neglected surrogate of a man and his wife, treated contemptuously. But God loved Hagar, and He sought her out, promising good for her life. Hagar called Him "*the God who sees me.*"

In times of deep distress, we may not have the words, or even the will, to pray. But the Holy Spirit prays for us.

> *And the Holy Spirit helps us in our weakness. For example, we do not know what God wants us to pray for. But the Holy Spirit prays for us with groanings that cannot be expressed in words. And the Father who knows all hearts knows what the Spirit is saying, for the Spirit pleads for us believers in harmony with God's own will. And we know that God causes everything to work together for the good of those who love God and are called according to his purpose for them.* (Romans 8:26–28 NLT)

Supplication is a term we rarely use in our daily lives. It means to humbly request something from God. Because intercession involves praying for others, we can treat supplication as prayers for our own needs and our own character growth.

What a special relationship we have with our God, who sees us. Even when our pain is great or life is overwhelming, God hears the wordless cry of our hearts. He seeks us out, guiding, strengthening, and blessing us. And He works everything together for the good of all who love Him.

Pray: *Lord, You are the God who sees me. Sometimes, I can only cry out or groan. Yet I know You hear my sorrow and my confusion. You strengthen me in my weakness. I trust You will bring the events of my life about for my good and Your glory. Amen!*

DAY 24

POURING OUT MY SOUL TO THE LORD

In her deep anguish Hannah prayed to the Lord, *weeping bitterly.* (1 Samuel 1:10 NIV)

Read: 1 Samuel 1:9–20

Have you ever prayed so hard that someone else thought you might be drunk? Pouring our souls out to God is the correct response to moments of great anguish, desire, or uncertainty in our lives. Just as we sometimes have only groans to offer the Lord, at other times, we have all the words, all at once. God understands that too.

Hannah longed to have a child. In fact, she wanted a child so badly, she promised to dedicate the son she asked God for as a special servant to the Lord. Then, Hannah's prayer devolved into silently mouthing so many words that the prophet Eli rebuked her for having too much wine. What she actually had was a whole lot of pain, anxiety, and grief. She promised Eli she was praying rightly, so he said, "*Go in peace, and may the God of Israel grant you what you have asked of him*" (1 Samuel 1:17 NIV). After pouring out her soul to the Lord, Hannah was able to go home in peace. She was no longer sad, and the next morning, she worshipped God.

God granted Hannah's request, giving her a son named Samuel. In return, Hannah kept her promise to God, later bringing the boy to the temple to live and serve the Lord. Samuel grew to become the final leader and prophet of Israel before God's people began appointing kings. Through God's gift of Samuel, Hannah was blessed. The nation of Israel gained a faithful and godly leader. And God Himself was glorified.

It is important to note that we don't bargain with God when we pray. In fact, God doesn't answer our prayers because we use the right words or pray in the correct manner. Instead, the Lord meets our needs according to His will.

John writes, *"This is the confidence we have in approaching God: that if we ask anything according to his will, he hears us. And if we know that he hears us—whatever we ask—we know that we have what we asked of him"* (1 John 5:14–15 NIV). God answers our prayers when they glorify Him, when they grow our character, and when they fit His plan for our lives and for the lives of those around us.

What is in your soul today? It is not too much for God. In fact, He cares about hearing from His children. The more you spend time in Scripture, the more you will find that your prayers align with God's will. Peace will come as you know the Lord hears you and as you trust that His answer will be what is best for you.

Pray: *Lord, thank You that I can pour out my heart to You. Help me not to make foolish vows, but to carefully consider any promise I make. Let me remember that You are working to grow my character and that You will be glorified through my life. I also want to bring You glory. Help me to pray in agreement with Your will for my life. Thank You for the peace that comes from bringing all my needs to You.*

DAY 25

REMEMBER ME, O GOD

Remember this good deed, O my God, and do not forget all that I have faithfully done for the Temple of my God and its services. (Nehemiah 13:14 NLT)

Read: Nehemiah 13:6–32

Have you worked for the Lord but encountered resistance from the people who were helping you in your labor for God? Perhaps you must remind yourself that your reward will not be here on earth but in eternity. As we live for Him, God remembers us.

Nehemiah, the cupbearer of the Persian king Artaxerxes, understood spiritual resistance. About one hundred and fifty years after the exile of Judah to Babylon, Nehemiah traveled to Jerusalem to help rebuild the walls and gates of the city. First, Nehemiah praised God and asked God to hear him. He confessed his sin and the sin of God's people. Then, Nehemiah asked God to grant him mercy and success.

God gave Nehemiah favor, first with Artaxerxes, who allowed him to rebuild Jerusalem's wall, and next with the people of Israel, who agreed to help with the reconstruction. The work was hard, and the people encountered opposition from their enemies. They struggled with discouragement and despair. Some Israelite nobles even refused to labor. Eventually, because of the constant threats, the people had to work in shifts with half of them building the wall while the other half stood guard against enemies with spears, shields, and bows.

Once the wall was finished, Nehemiah restored the worship of God to its correct place and order. God's law was read to the people. They celebrated God's Feast of Booths as families and publicly confessed their sin as a people. Then, the people dedicated the wall they had built to God and organized the service of the priests at the temple.

But the people were lax in their worship. There were pagans among the people of God, there was an enemy living in the storeroom of the temple, the priests were not being provided for, and the people were breaking the Old Covenant Sabbath law. Nehemiah returned to Jerusalem to reinstitute the proper worship of God. Three times, Nehemiah asked God to remember him.

There is no shame in wanting God to see the work we are doing for His kingdom. We too can ask God to remember us in our trials and struggles as we serve Him. James 1:12 (NIV) tells us, *"Blessed is the one who perseveres under trial because, having stood the test, that person will receive the crown of life that the Lord has promised to those who love him."*

We can rest in the truth that our trials are merely a test. When we persevere in serving the Lord, God will remember us when we come into His kingdom. There is a reward—a crown of life—waiting for those who love Jesus.

Pray: *Lord, one day You will reward us based on how we have served You. Remember me for the deeds of faithful love I have done for You, for Your church, and to further the church's faithful worship of You. Help me remember my reward is not here on earth, but in heaven. Let me endure any trials as though they are merely a test. Help me pass every test and one day receive the crown of life.*

DAY 26

LEAD ME IN YOUR TRUTH

Lead me in your truth and teach me, for you are the God of my salvation; for you I wait all the day long. (Psalm 25:5)

Read: Psalm 25

Have you ever wondered if it is right to pray for yourself? When it comes time for prayer requests in your Bible study or Sunday School class, maybe you've heard others say something like, "I don't want prayer for me, but my neighbor needs our attention." God, though, wants us to ask Him for help.

The Psalms are a wonderful place to find biblical prayers. In fact, when we pray straight from the Bible, we are addressing God with the very words He gave us to use. It is right to go to our Father God with our needs, just as David did in Psalm 25, a prayer asking for God's hand on his life. David's prayer alternates between praising God for His wonderful attributes and asking for help.

First, David praises God as the one who is worthy of his trust. God never puts His people to shame, but instead saves them through His mercy, steadfast love, and faithfulness. He is good and upright. God never abandons us to confusion, but guides us as we follow Him, instructing us through His Word. God offers us friendship, and He rescues us.

Then, David asks God to keep him from shame or from the pain of his enemies rejoicing over his situation. He asks God to teach him truth and to lead him in the way he should go. David also asks God to save him, forgetting his sins and pardoning him from punishment. He pleads with God to be gracious to him and to bring him out of his distress, his loneliness, and his affliction. Last, David asks God to guard his soul, deliver him, and help him live with integrity and uprightness.

Psalm 25:14 says, "*The friendship of the* Lord *is for those who fear him, and he makes known to them his covenant.*" God offers His friendship to those who honor and respect Him as Lord. We can go to Him with our worries, our concerns, and our troubles. We can trust in Him, for He is steadfast, showing us loving-kindness.

Walking a life of righteousness is not easy. We love our people, yet responding graciously in love is a legitimate struggle. Instead, the screeching cry of a toddler or the questioning challenge of a teen can be an instant temptation to respond in anger. God welcomes your prayers for patience, a quiet spirit, and self-control.

Pray: *Lord, You are good and loving. I trust You. Please lead me in Your truth and teach me. I want to grow in my knowledge of You. You are the God of my salvation, and I wait for You all day long. Help me to honor and respect You, to humbly follow Your way. When I am lonely and troubled, help me to turn to You. Please turn to me and deliver me from my problems. May I always live before You with integrity and righteousness.*

DAY 27

HELP MY UNBELIEF!

Immediately the father of the child cried out and said with tears, "Lord, I believe; help my unbelief!"

(Mark 9:24 NKJV)

Read: Mark 9:14–29

Have you ever found yourself praying as if God is not truly capable of answering? Maybe you feel like God is not listening. After all, not everything is going the way you think it should. Thankfully, God helps us with our unbelief.

The truth is that God sometimes says *no* to our requests because we come to Him with the wrong motive. We can be double-minded, proud, or seeking only our own desires. We might ignore the will of God in our prayer, or we may be involved in active sin. (See James 4:1–10.) Sometimes, though, we lack faith, as the disciples did when they asked God to heal a boy of his demon possession.

Sometimes God grows our faith—our trust in Him—by allowing us to develop perseverance in prayer. In the case of the man with the tormented son, *"Jesus said to him, 'If you can believe, all things are possible to him who believes'"* (Mark 9:23 NKJV). The man responded with the faith he had in Jesus, "Lord, I believe!" Immediately, he realized he was in need of even more faith, so he cried out, *"Help my unbelief!"*

Exactly what is faith? Hebrews 11:1 (NKJV) tells us, *"Now faith is the substance of things hoped for, the evidence of things not seen."* In the Old Testament, people were saved through their faith in God's promise of the coming Messiah. Under the new covenant that Jesus ushered in, we have faith that Jesus is the Son of God and God the Son. We believe in faith that He came to die for our sins and He rose again from the dead. We also have faith that Jesus will one day return for His people, setting all things right. We trust God and we believe in His promises.

Jesus told the disciples, *"And whatever things you ask in prayer, believing, you will receive"* (Matthew 21:22 NKJV). John tells us that when we ask God for something according to His will, He hears us and answers us. (See 1 John 5:14–15.) As we pray to the Lord, it is good to recognize that even our faith in Jesus comes from Him. After Peter healed a lame man, he spoke to the witnesses about the name of Jesus, saying, *"And His name, through faith in His name, has made this man strong, whom you see and know. Yes, the faith which comes through Him has given him this perfect soundness in the presence of you all"* (Acts 3:16 NKJV).

The very faith we have in Jesus is given to us by Jesus Himself. If you find yourself lacking in faith, ask Jesus to help your unbelief. The power, glory, and might are all His.

Pray: *Jesus, I believe in You. I believe. Yet help me in my unbelief. Chase from me any doubt in Your goodness, mercy, grace, and power over all. Remind me that You are sovereign, and You care about the events of my life. Help me to remember that my faith grows through prayer and fasting. Let me ask for Your will to be done.*

DAY 28

GRANT US BOLDNESS

And now, O Lord, hear their threats, and give us, your servants, great boldness in preaching your word.

(Acts 4:29 NLT)

Read: Acts 4:23–31

Have you ever hesitated to share the gospel? Perhaps you don't want to be mocked or disregarded. These are common fears, but God gives us boldness to share the good news of Jesus with others.

In the days and years after Jesus was crucified, resurrected, and ascended to heaven, the apostles went forth and shared the gospel. For their efforts, they were beaten, jailed, and even martyred. Yet their prayers reflected their faith in Jesus. Rather than praying for safety, comfort, or even justice, they asked God for boldness to speak the truth about God's plan for salvation.

Early in their ministry, Peter and John stood in the temple square as Peter called people to repent and follow Jesus. Over five thousand men—and perhaps as many women—were saved as they heard and believed God's Word. The priests and Sadducees hauled Peter and John off to jail, before warning the men not to speak in the name of Jesus again and releasing them the next day. Courageously, the apostles replied, *"Whether it is right in the sight of God to listen to you more than to God, you judge. For we cannot but speak the things which we have seen and heard"* (Acts 4:19–20 NKJV).

When the apostles and their friends gathered together later that day, the first thing they did was pray. They began by praising God as the sovereign Creator. Then, they recognized that persecution for speaking the name of Jesus is nothing new, and they remembered that it was according to God's plan for our salvation that Jesus was crucified. Next, the believers asked God to give them boldness and confidence to speak His Word to others. They confessed that it was through the name of Jesus and the hand of God that a man was healed the day before. It was a sign and wonder to point to the power of Jesus.

Peter, John, and their friends didn't ask God to protect them from the consequences of their faith. Instead, they asked God for boldness and confidence to share the truth from Scripture. They asked in faith, aligned with God's will. In return, the Holy Spirit gave them the boldness they sought. Acts 4:31 (NKJV) says, *"And when they had prayed, the place where they were assembled together was shaken; and they were all filled with the Holy Spirit, and they spoke the word of God with boldness."*

It can be easy for us to decide that sharing the gospel is someone else's spiritual gifting. Instead, we should each follow the example of the disciples and ask God to grant us boldness. The people around us need Jesus. We just need the courage to share God's message with them.

Pray: *Lord, speaking Your Word and sharing the gospel of Jesus comes with the threat of disapproval—and even danger—here on this earth. Yet, I desire to share the good news of Jesus with others. I know this is Your will for me in Christ Jesus. Let me be Your servant and grant me confidence and boldness to share the gospel without fear.*

DAY 29

MAY WE DO HIS WILL

Now may the God of peace who brought again from the dead our Lord Jesus, the great shepherd of the sheep, by the blood of the eternal covenant, equip you with everything good that you may do his will, working in us that which is pleasing in his sight, through Jesus Christ, to whom be glory forever and ever. Amen. (Hebrews 13:20–21)

Read: Hebrews 13

Do you ever read the New Testament and wonder how you can live up to the commands for believers or know what God's will is? There is no need for concern. When we ask Him, God equips us to live for Him.

The book of Hebrews ends with encouragement to offer a sacrifice of praise and service to God. Hebrews 13 explains how the Old Testament sacrificial system and the tabernacle pointed to the coming of Jesus. God taught the Israelites to worship Him in a way that foreshadowed the sacrifice Jesus would one day make for us on the cross. Today, rather than sacrificing animals outside the camp, we trust that Jesus shed His blood at Calvary in payment for our sin.

Because we follow Jesus, we live a life separated from the world. Our testimony to Christ's redeeming power is the way we serve Him. We love our sisters and brothers in Christ, and we treat strangers, prisoners, and the abused with hospitality. We remain faithful in marriage. We are also content with the Lord's provision, not falling into a love of money.

Hebrews 13:8 says, *"Jesus Christ is the same yesterday and today and forever."* Remembering that our Lord and His message do not change, we stay away from novel or false teaching. Instead, we honor and care for our pastors and elders, submitting to their leadership, and seeking to imitate their good example of the faith.

We praise God with our mouths, and we share what we have with others. Ephesians 2:10 says, *"For we are his workmanship, created in Christ Jesus for good works, which God prepared beforehand, that we should walk in them."* God determined the good deeds He has for you to do before you were ever born, and He has equipped you to bring glory to Him.

The author of Hebrews ends the list of living sacrifices we offer our King with a benediction, a prayer asking God to bless, help, and protect us. God raised Jesus from the dead, and Jesus's blood marks the new covenant. Because of the sacrifice Jesus made to pay the debt for our sins, we are saved by grace through faith. (See Ephesians 2:8.)

Serving the Lord is a pleasure. We can ask God to equip us to do every good thing that God's will requires of us. That way, our lives will be pleasing in the sight of God.

Pray: *Lord, You truly are the God of peace. You resurrected Jesus from the dead after He died to pay for my sin. Jesus is the Good Shepherd, and I am His sheep. Please equip me to do every good thing according to Your will. Help me to carry out the good works You have ordained just for me. May I bring Jesus glory and honor and praise all the days of my life.*

PRAYERS OF INTERCESSION

For this reason we also, since the day we heard it, do not cease to pray for you, and to ask that you may be filled with the knowledge of His will in all wisdom and spiritual understanding; that you may walk worthy of the Lord, fully pleasing Him, being fruitful in every good work and increasing in the knowledge of God.

—Colossians 1:9–10 NKJV

We ask God to meet the needs of others.

DAY 30

MAY MY CHILD LIVE BEFORE YOU

And Abraham said to God, "Oh that Ishmael might live before you!" (Genesis 17:18)

Read: Genesis 17:15–21

Have you ever prayed for your child's salvation? Of all the people we can pray for, perhaps we pray most earnestly for our kids. Because we know that *"salvation belongs to the LORD"* (Jonah 2:9), we can trust that God is exactly who we should bring our concerns to, for God cares about our kids.

In Genesis 17, God comes to ninety-nine-year-old Abraham and promises to make him the father of kings and nations. Then, He vows to be the God of Abraham's heirs forever. Finally, God promises to give Abraham and his offspring the land of Canaan as an everlasting possession. This covenant—this binding promise from God—was to be sealed with the circumcision of every male in Abraham's household. It didn't matter if the boys and men were servants or blood relatives of Abraham, or whether they were Jewish or foreign-born. Every single male under Abraham's care was to be circumcised to show that God was their God.

Abraham laughed at the idea that he would be the father of nations. After all, his wife, Sarah, was too old to have a child. But Abraham already had a son by Sarah's Egyptian servant, Hagar. So he prayed to God, *"Oh that Ishmael might live before you!"* Maybe Abraham thought his line of kings and nations could come from his thirteen-year-old son, Ishmael. Perhaps the Lord would honor Abraham's son, even though Abraham and Sarah had taken the fulfillment of God's promise into their own hands, creating a child outside their wedding vows.

Yet God said *no* to Abraham's request that Ishmael be the heir through whom all of God's promises were fulfilled. Instead, God's everlasting covenant with the soon-to-exist nation of Israel would be with the children and grandchildren of Isaac, who would be born to Abraham and Sarah the following year. Just because Ishmael was born outside God's covenant with Abraham, though, did not mean God forgot him. This child, born to a servant and despised by Sarah, was prayed for by his father. God heard Abraham and replied, *"As for Ishmael, I have heard you; behold, I have blessed him and will make him fruitful and multiply him greatly. He shall father twelve princes, and I will make him into a great nation"* (Genesis 17:20).

We love our children. Yet God loves them even more, and He has a plan for their lives. We can't circumvent or improve on God's plans, even when His promises seem impossible to us. Instead, we can go to God in prayer for our kids. God hears you when you bring the needs of your children and grandchildren before Him. What a relief it is to know that salvation belongs to the Lord. You can trust that our God, who is mighty to save, hears your prayers.

Pray: *Oh, Lord, may my children and grandchildren live before You. May they come to salvation in You and may their sin be removed from them. Help me to pray for my children, even when I am discouraged. Let my heart toward them be kind, loving, and forgiving, just as Your heart is toward me.*

DAY 31

REMEMBER YOUR PROMISES

But Moses sought the favor of the LORD his God. "LORD," he said, "why should your anger burn against your people, whom you brought out of Egypt with great power and a mighty hand?" (Exodus 32:11 NIV)

Read: Exodus 32:1–14

Have you ever wondered if your prayers for others matter? After all, we know God does not change His mind once He has made an unconditional declaration. (See Numbers 23:19.) Yet we pray to the God who changes history. Sometimes, God announces His intention to act, warning us to turn away from sin. When God warns, rather than declares, He allows the prayers of His righteous people to change the course of events. God wants us to seek Him in prayer, and He responds to our requests.

Psalm 106:20–23 (NIV) retells the story of the people of Israel asking Aaron to build them an idol—a golden calf—and of Moses's intercession for the people:

> *They exchanged their glorious God for an image of a bull, which eats grass. They forgot the God who saved them, who had done great things in Egypt, miracles in the land of Ham and awesome deeds by the Red Sea. So he said he would destroy them—had not Moses, his chosen one, stood in the breach before him to keep his wrath from destroying them.*

Moses reminded God of His character as a God of mercy and grace. Next, Moses remembered how God rescued His people from Egypt. Then, Moses appealed to God to remember His promise to Abraham, Isaac, and Jacob to bring the people to a promised land and to multiply them in number. Finally, Moses asked God, again, to have mercy on His people.

Because Moses prayed in response to God's announced anger, God spared the Israelites as a people. God still judged the people for their sin against Him, and some died by the sword or by plague. But God did not consume the entire nation as He warned He would. Instead, God heard Moses when he stood in the breach, interceding for God's people.

Nothing we do can earn the mercy and grace of God. Because God is holy, it takes only one sin to separate us from Him. Yet God is also loving, kind, steadfast, merciful, and patient. When we praise God for His attributes, we remind ourselves who He is, and we appeal to His nature. God will never act in a way that is contrary to who He is or what He has purposed.

Is there someone you need to stand in the gap for? Perhaps you are praying for someone who has turned from God. Maybe you are praying for your town, your school district and its students, your church, or your nation. Don't grow weary of doing good. God hears your prayers. Sometimes He even changes the course of history because of them.

Pray: *Lord, thank You for hearing my prayer. Remember Your grace, love, and mercy. Please turn from Your fierce anger and do not bring disaster on Your people. Instead, please help them to walk with You again. Help me not grow weary of doing good in prayer. Instead, let me stand in the gap for those who have forgotten to pray to You themselves.*

DAY 32

FORGIVE THEIR FOLLY

My servant Job will pray for you, and I will accept his prayer on your behalf. I will not treat you as you deserve, for you have not spoken accurately about me, as my servant Job has. (Job 42:8 NLT)

Read: Job 42:1–10

Have you ever wondered why the Lord allowed a time of pain in your life? During your suffering, perhaps the people around you even offered advice that hurt you further. Though it can seem unnatural, God wants us to pray for those who harm us.

Job was a righteous man who prayed for his children often, asking God to forgive their sins. Yet, in one day, Job lost all his servants, his oxen, donkeys, sheep, and camels, and then all his sons and daughters. As a final insult, Job was even covered in painful boils.

Rather than accusing our sovereign God of evil, Job worshipped Him, saying:

I came naked from my mother's womb, and I will be naked when I leave. The LORD gave me what I had, and the LORD has taken it away. Praise the name of the LORD! (Job 1:21 NLT)

When Job's friends came to comfort him, they each used basic biblical truths to blame Job for his own pain. After all, they reasoned, if Job was suffering this much, there must be some hidden sin in his life. As Bible readers, we know that Job was not to blame for his tragedy. Rather, God pointed Job out to Satan as a righteous man who feared God. Then, God gave Satan permission to test Job's faith.

Rather than cursing God, Job wanted to stand before God, to hear from Him. In fact, he demanded an audience with God. So God asked Job if he knew how God's creation was made, or if he could care for it, and whether Job had the wisdom and power to understand God's sovereign plan:

> *Brace yourself like a man; I will question you, and you shall answer me. Would you discredit my justice? Would you condemn me to justify yourself?* (Job 40:7–8 NIV)

Job quickly realized he had assumed too much about God's plan and His motives. God is God, the Creator of the heavens and earth, the ruler of the nations. So Job submitted to God's plan and his relationship with God was once again whole and good. God, though, rebuked Job's friends for speaking for God. He called Job's friends to repent, telling them His servant Job would pray for them. How humbling that must have been for them!

Perhaps you have had times of great struggle, when those who should have comforted you have hurt you instead. Maybe they made assumptions about your relationship with God. It is possible you've been blamed for tragedy in your life. Jesus tells us, *"But I say to you, Love your enemies and pray for those who persecute you"* (Matthew 5:44). Like Job, our God-given job is to pray for others, even for those who harm us.

Pray: *Lord, You are so good, and Your plan is best for me. Help me to speak the truth about You even in times of trouble. Help me, too, to pray for those who harm me. There are people who take joy in my suffering. Let me be faithful to pray for their good and for their repentance.*

DAY 33

HAVE MERCY, O LORD

A Gentile woman who lived there came to him, pleading, "Have mercy on me, O Lord, Son of David! For my daughter is possessed by a demon that torments her severely."
(Matthew 15:22 NLT)

Read: Matthew 15:21–28

Have you ever wondered how long you should pray for someone you love? It can seem like you pray and pray, yet nothing happens. Maybe the situation even gets worse. Yet God calls us to persevere in prayer.

The story of the gentile woman pleading with Jesus to save her daughter can seem jarring. Imagine the agony she felt, watching her daughter tormented day after day by an evil spirit. The woman called Jesus, *"Lord, Son of David,"* the title of a man descended from a king. She had likely heard that Jesus could heal, so she came to Him to beg for the restoration of her daughter.

In response, the disciples asked Jesus to send the bothersome gentile woman away. Jesus did not answer her at first. Then He told her, *"I was sent only to help God's lost sheep—the people of Israel"* (Matthew 15:24 NLT). After all, God's plan for salvation was to extend grace first to His chosen people, the Israelites, then to the gentiles. (See Romans 15:8–9.) Yet the woman knelt before Jesus in a position of worship and begged Him to help her. That is when Jesus told her that it is not right to throw the children's food to the dogs.

This harsh statement seems like an insult, but Jesus was testing the woman's faith in Him. Sometimes, God delays in answering our prayers in order to help us grow and develop our trust in Him. When we are faced with silence, we must decide whether we will continue to seek help from God, trusting Him to answer our pleas, or take our problems into our own hands.

The disciples were ready to discount the Canaanite woman's pleas altogether, simply because she did not fit their idea of who could seek Jesus's help. The woman, though, was not easily offended. Instead, she showed great humility as she replied that even dogs are allowed to eat the scraps that fall under the table of their masters. For her persistence, Jesus rewarded the woman, telling her that her faith was great and her request was granted. Imagine the joy she felt when her daughter was healed of the demon that had plagued her.

When you wonder if you should continue to pray for a request that seems to go unanswered, remember that Colossians 4:2 (NLT) says, *"Devote yourselves to prayer with an alert mind and a thankful heart."* God calls us to persevere in prayer—to endure, persist, and press on—as we devote ourselves to seeking Christ. Remember that while the Lord values our faith and our humility, He also cares about our perseverance.

Pray: *Lord, have mercy on me and on those I love. Please deliver my family and friends from evil. Help me to persevere in prayer, devoted to seeking You with an alert mind and a thankful heart. Help me to remain humble when You test me. Let my commitment to come to You with my concerns for others one day be a testimony to my faith in You.*

DAY 34

MAKE HER WELL

And begged Him earnestly, saying, "My little daughter lies at the point of death. Come and lay Your hands on her, that she may be healed, and she will live." (Mark 5:23 NKJV)

Read: Mark 5:21–24, 35–43

Have you found yourself facing true fear and doubt as you pray? Maybe someone you love is sick or in danger, and your only hope for their restoration or safety is that God will rescue them. You may wonder, "What if God says no?" Thankfully, our God is compassionate toward us.

Jairus, a ruler of the synagogue, was earnest and humble; he had faith that his twelve-year-old girl would live if only Jesus would lay His hands on her. So he fell at Jesus's feet, begging Him to save his dying daughter. From our perspective, Jairus did everything right. As Jesus and Jairus made their way through a crowd that pressed around Him, Jesus was delayed by another faith-filled woman who sought healing. They were on their way to the sick girl when an official came from Jairus's house, telling him not to bother Jesus, for his daughter had died.

Jesus told Jairus, *"Do not be afraid; only believe"* (Mark 5:36 NKJV). Though she had died, Jesus raised Jairus's daughter to life, healed and well, while bystanders mocked Him. Our Lord showed compassion to Jairus and his wife, the little girl's mother, taking them with Him and His disciples while He told the child to rise. After she began walking around, Jesus showed compassion to the girl, telling her parents to give her food to eat.

God does sometimes answer our sincere and faith-filled prayers with a *no*. Other times, He makes us wait for His response. Though believers will one day live in eternity with Jesus, life in this broken world often holds suffering, pain, and even death. Yet God's plan for us is always best. In fact, Romans 5:3–5 tells us to rejoice in our sufferings for God uses our pain to produce endurance, character, and hope in our lives.

When we worry that Jesus may not answer or even hear our desperate prayer for someone we love, fear is often our first response. Anxiety, though, is not the proper response to our concerns. As Paul writes, "*For the Spirit God gave us does not make us timid, but gives us power, love and self-discipline*" (2 Timothy 1:7 NIV).

When we come to Jesus with our deeply important requests for others, we remember that Jesus is a compassionate Savior. We remind ourselves, too, that our God has given us a spirit of power, love, and self-discipline. You can, in fact, rejoice in suffering, knowing that God is growing your endurance, your character, and your hope in Him. That is what He is doing for your loved ones as well.

Pray: *Lord, please pay attention to the people I love who are suffering. I believe that You can do anything, and I know that You can bring them safety and healing. I also know that You are using their pain to grow endurance, character, and hope in my life and theirs. Help me not to fear, for You have given me a spirit of power, love, and self-discipline.*

DAY 35

PRAYING FOR GOD'S SALVATION PLAN

She did not depart from the temple, worshiping with fasting and prayer night and day. (Luke 2:37)

Read: Luke 2:36–38

Have you ever grown weary of praying for someone? Perhaps you have found that other obligations distract you from praying for them for days or even weeks. Yet, God calls us to be constant in our prayers.

Anna prayed patiently and consistently for a long time. In fact, after her husband died following just seven years of marriage, Anna stayed at the temple, worshipping God night and day through fasting and prayer. After five or six decades of Anna's prayers offered continually to the Lord, Jesus Christ was born. God graciously allowed her to see the arrival of His promised Messiah.

Forty days after Jesus's birth, Mary and Joseph brought their baby to the temple in Jerusalem so they could offer the required sacrifice. Simeon, a righteous man who was also praying and waiting for the Christ, followed the Holy Spirit's leading to the temple, where he prayed over Jesus. Anna, too, met Jesus at the temple. She gave thanks to God and told everyone there about God's redemption through Jesus, the Messiah.

After dozens of years of praying, Anna was allowed to witness the arrival of Jesus, God the Son, born to be fully God and fully human. What a joy that must have been for her. Praying with perseverance while waiting patiently for the Lord is not an easy task, but the reward is real.

In fact, waiting in prayer is like planting squash seeds. It can take weeks to see even the smallest sprout. More time passes as the vine grows and puts out flowers. Eventually, squash appear, but there's still more waiting to do before they are ready to be picked and eaten. Paul reminds us, *"And let us not grow weary of doing good, for in due season we will reap, if we do not give up. So then, as we have opportunity, let us do good to everyone, and especially to those who are of the household of faith"* (Galatians 6:9–10).

When people are in need, we tend to think of making a meal or running to the grocery store as a practical way to *do good* for them. There is nothing quite as important, though, as continuing to bring someone before the throne of grace. Our Christ, Jesus, is able to do everything needed to change the situation of those we pray for.

So when you grow weary of *just* praying, think of Anna, who dedicated her life to prayer. Remember the seeds you are sowing, which God will one day cause to bear fruit. Remind yourself, too, of Romans 12:12: *"Rejoice in hope, be patient in tribulation, be constant in prayer."*

Pray: *Lord, thank You for the coming of Jesus. Thank You also for Anna, who prayed night and day for Your salvation plan. Help me to never grow weary of doing good. Let me pray faithfully for everyone, especially those who are in the household of faith. I want to rejoice in hope, wait patiently for Your answer in tribulation, and be constant in prayer, knowing You hear me and You are working in the lives and circumstances of those I'm praying for.*

DAY 36

WALK WORTHY OF THE LORD

For this reason, since the day we heard about you, we have not stopped praying for you. We continually ask God to fill you with the knowledge of his will through all the wisdom and understanding that the Spirit gives.

(Colossians 1:9 NIV)

Read: Colossians 1:3–14

Do you ever find yourself at a loss over what to pray for a fellow Christian? Perhaps you struggle to pray for anything beyond salvation, health, blessings, or safety. God wants you to lift fellow believers in prayer, and Paul gives us a wonderful prayer list in Colossians 1:3–14.

Paul wrote his letter to the people of Colossae while imprisoned in Rome. He extensively gave thanks for his fellow sisters and brothers in Christ and for God's work in their lives. In fact, he begins and ends his prayer with thanksgiving to God.

Following Paul's example, you can thank God for a fellow believer's faith in Jesus and her love for all God's people. You can also thank God that she heard and understood the gospel. In fact, praise our sovereign Lord that the gospel is spreading throughout the world. Prayer is a conversation with God, so do not hesitate to joyfully follow the leading of the Holy Spirit, praying for everyone He brings to mind. Paul did just that as he remembered Epaphras, who first shared the gospel with the Colossians. You can praise God, too, for giving your spiritual sister an inheritance in His kingdom. God rescued your friend or family member from the kingdom of darkness and brought her into the kingdom of His Son. Thank God for her redemption. Her sins are forgiven!

God has done much for your sister in Christ already, but you can intercede for her without mentioning even one specific circumstance in her life. Instead, pray for her to learn more about God and His will. Then, ask God to give her wisdom and understanding through the Holy Spirit. Next, ask God to help her live a life worthy of the Lord, pleasing God as she bears spiritual fruit, doing every good work God gives her to do. Last, ask God to strengthen her with power through His glorious might, giving her endurance and patience in His strength.

How should you pray for your fellow believers? God's Word tells us to pray continually. Anytime you think of someone, or when you see a friend or church member on social media, take a moment to thank God for their salvation and to pray for their spiritual growth. It is an act of love they may never know about, but God certainly hears you as you pray.

Pray: *Lord, help me to never stop praying for my fellow believers. I want to continually ask You, Lord, to fill them with the knowledge of Your will through the wisdom and understanding that comes from the Holy Spirit, through prayer and the reading of Your Word. Help my loved ones to live lives that honor You. Strengthen them by Your power, giving them endurance and patience. Thank You so much for the good news of Jesus, which leads to salvation and the forgiveness of sins!*

DAY 37

LET THE GOSPEL GO FORTH

We give thanks to God always for all of you, constantly mentioning you in our prayers, remembering before our God and Father your work of faith and labor of love and steadfastness of hope in our Lord Jesus Christ.

(1 Thessalonians 1:2–3)

Read: 1 Thessalonians 1:2–10

Do you pray for your church? We often remember to pray for a fellow believer when they are suffering greatly. It is a good thing to meet together regularly with our church body to pray for the nation or for our community. God also wants us to pray for the body of Christ at the church we attend.

Galatians 6:2 says it this way: "*Bear one another's burdens, and so fulfill the law of Christ.*" We bear each other's burdens individually and we also pray for the body of Christ as a whole. Our fellowship—those we worship with weekly—needs our prayers.

In the beginning of his first letter to the church at Thessalonica, Paul describes how he, Silas, and Timothy pray for the congregation. This description offers us another model for praying for our sisters and brothers in Christ. As you follow Paul's example in prayer, there are a number of things you can pray for the members of your church.

You can begin your prayer by thanking God that your church members work for the Lord in faith and in love. Thank God that they persevere in their hope in Jesus Christ, in the presence of our Father God who chose them for salvation. You can thank God, too, that the gospel came to their lives in the power of the Holy Spirit. Praise God for those who cared enough to share the gospel with full conviction with each one of you.

Pray for the younger members of your church to imitate the faith and walk of members who are mature in the Lord. Ask God to help them become more like Jesus, growing spiritually as they live out their faith. Thank the Lord that even in their struggles, they received the gospel with the joy of the Holy Spirit.

Next, pray for the testimony of the men, women, and young people in your church. Their faithful service to the Lord will bear witness to God's saving grace as people in your community notice there is something authentic about the goodness, gentleness, and love of those who attend your church. Pray that those in your fellowship will turn from idolatry to the living God. Finally, ask God to help your sisters and brothers in Christ faithfully wait for Jesus to return from heaven for His people. Jesus rescues each believer from the wrath of God on the day of judgment.

Pray: *Father, help me always thank You for everyone in my church body. Help me always mention those I fellowship with in my prayers. Let me remember their works of faith and their labors of love. I see the way they persevere in their hope in Jesus, worshipping in the presence of You, Father. Let me love the body of Christ You have placed me in and help us to be an attractive witness to Your love and mercy.*

PRAYERS OF DELIVERANCE

When the righteous cry for help, the Lord hears and delivers them out of all their troubles.
—Psalm 34:17

We cry out to God for help in times of trouble.

DAY 38
SAVE MY CHILD

Then she went and sat down across from him at a distance of about a bowshot; for she said to herself, "Let me not see the death of the boy." So she sat opposite him, and lifted her voice and wept. (Genesis 21:16 NKJV)

Read: Genesis 21:8–21

Have you ever seen disaster coming and panicked before it ever arrived? Maybe your child was sick, your bills were outsized, or your car showed signs of its imminent demise. There have likely been times in your life when you knew you needed deliverance. It is an amazing fact that God hears our tears.

When Isaac was maybe two or three years old, Abraham and Sarah had a feast to celebrate the day he was weaned. On that day, Sarah saw Hagar's son, Ishmael, scoffing. Enraged, she demanded that Abraham cast Hagar and her son out of the camp so that Ishmael wouldn't have a share of Isaac's inheritance. God had already promised that Isaac was to be Abraham's heir. So God told Abraham to send Hagar and Ishmael away, as Sarah demanded.

This put Hagar in a seemingly impossible situation. Early the next morning, Abraham gave her bread and a skin full of water. Then he sent her into the wilderness of Beersheba with her sixteen-year-old son. Hagar had nowhere to go and no one to ask for help. When their water ran out, Hagar had her beloved teen sit under the shade of a bush. She went a good distance from him and declared she did not want to witness the death of her boy. Then, she wept loudly.

Hagar could not see hope in her situation. Rather than pray, or even look for a well, she gave up. Yet God heard her cries. *"And God heard the voice of the lad"* (Genesis 21:17 NKJV). It seems that Ishmael was praying too, perhaps as Hagar taught him.

For the second time in her life, Hagar was visited by the angel of God, who called to her from heaven. He asked her what was wrong, told her not to fear, and assured her that God heard Ishmael's voice. He told her to rise, to help Ishmael up, and to hold onto him by the hand. God promised He would make Ishmael into a great nation and opened Hagar's eyes so she could see a well nearby. He answered Hagar's desperate need before she even asked Him, providing for her before she saw the provision. God heard her cry and delivered her.

Psalm 34:17 (NKJV) says, *"The righteous cry out, and the LORD hears, and delivers them out of all their troubles."* When we love God, the Lord hears our tears as a cry for help. When you run out of hope and words, cry out to God, who hears your tears. It just may be that He has provided for you before you can even see the provision coming.

Pray: *God, Psalm 56:8 (NKJV) says,* "You number my wanderings; put my tears into Your bottle; are they not in Your book?" *Lord, I see disaster coming, and I don't want to go through it. I am overcome by fear and grief. Yet I know that You provide for Your people. Please hear my cry and care for my needs.*

DAY 39

GOD HEARD THEIR GROANING

God heard their groaning, and God remembered his covenant with Abraham, with Isaac, and with Jacob.
(Exodus 2:24)

Read: Exodus 2:23–25

Do you ever wonder if you are the only one praying about a terrible situation? Perhaps you see something occurring in your nation or community and you feel as though you are the only one who cares. Be assured, God knows our pain.

The Hebrew women enslaved in the land of Egypt probably felt alone in their situation too. More than four hundred years earlier, Joseph, who had been sold into slavery by his brothers, saved them and their families from famine by having them settle in the Nile River delta region of Egypt. The land was beautiful, there was plenty of food, and they settled down with their cattle and sheep.

Four centuries later, those seventy family members had grown into a nation of more than six hundred thousand men between the ages of twenty and sixty. Yet their good home had begun to seem like a prison. There had been new pharaoh after new pharaoh, and the good work Joseph had done to preserve the Egyptians during the famine was forgotten. Instead, the current pharaoh saw a nation of around two million people inside his borders, and he enslaved them.

Forced to make mud bricks to build storage cities in the hot sun, under harsh taskmasters, the people continued to multiply.

To weaken the people of Israel, Pharaoh ordered the killing of all Hebrew baby boys. When the Israelite midwives refused to kill the babies, the evil king ordered his own people to throw every Hebrew baby boy into the Nile.

It was into this tragic moment that Moses was born. God saved his life, arranging events so that he was raised by Pharaoh's own daughter. Eighty years after Pharaoh issued a death sentence for the Israelite boys, Moses was living in the wilderness as a shepherd. The people of Egypt groaned in the midst of their slavery and called out to God.

God heard the groaning of the people. He remembered the promises He made to Abraham, Isaac, and Jacob—their ancestors. Then, God sent Moses and his brother, Aaron, to help rescue the people of Israel. God had been arranging the events of history for the rescue of His people long before they ever groaned.

There are times when it feels like we alone are bringing our situation before God. The Israelites were not gathering to cry out in corporate prayer, yet the groans of the people were rising to God to create a collective cry. Peter writes, "*The eyes of the Lord are on the righteous, and his ears are open to their prayer. But the face of the Lord is against those who do evil*" (1 Peter 3:12).

When you call out to the Lord over injustice, oppression, or just plain evil, remember that He hears your groaning. He sees you, He remembers you, and He knows your pain.

Pray: *Lord, hear my cry for help and remember Your promises to me. Open Your ears to the request of Your righteous people. Save us from evil. Help me to trust that You ordain the events of my life.*

DAY 40

OPEN HIS EYES TO YOUR DELIVERANCE

And Elisha prayed, and said, "LORD, I pray, open his eyes that he may see." Then the LORD opened the eyes of the young man, and he saw. And behold, the mountain was full of horses and chariots of fire all around Elisha.

(2 Kings 6:17 NKJV)

Read: 2 Kings 6:8–23

Do you ever despair of receiving help from the Lord? Perhaps it seems like God is not even paying attention. Yet God is already working to accomplish His purpose.

The prophet Elisha's servant felt hopeless when he woke early one morning and looked out over the wall of the city to see charioteers and infantry men, chariots and horses, all ready to breach the city walls or lay siege to the city. Imagine the panic he must have felt when he realized the Syrians had arrived to seize Elisha, who had been interfering with their plans to defeat Israel. Crying out to Elisha, the servant asked what in the world they should do. It seems like a strange question, doesn't it? After all, what could two men of God do against an entire army bent on their destruction?

Praying is exactly the right thing to do in hopeless moments of intense despair. Elisha had already been in contact with God. He knew that not only was there a plan, but God was already acting on that plan. Elisha told his servant, *"Do not be afraid, for those who are with us are more than those who are with them"* (2 Kings 6:16).

Indeed, when Elisha asked God to open the servant's eyes, the man suddenly saw the truth. All around them stood the army of God, complete with horses and chariots of fire. Led by the Holy Spirit, God's prophet prayed again, and the Syrian army was blinded. Elisha led the blind soldiers peacefully to the Israelite king in Samaria. Then, Elisha prayed a third time, and the Syrian army suddenly was able to see their predicament. They were stranded in enemy territory. Rather than striking them down, the king of Israel fed the Syrians and sent them home.

Colossians 1:16 says, *"For by him all things were created, in heaven and on earth, visible and invisible, whether thrones or dominions or rulers or authorities—all things were created through him and for him."* Jesus is the creator of both the world we can see, and the world we can't. That is a terrifying reality for those who don't follow Jesus. For believers, it is a wonderful truth.

The next time you pray for deliverance, remember Elisha's servant. He thought he saw the stark reality of his painful situation. Yet the Lord opened his eyes so he could see the spiritual world all around him. In your situation, too, the Lord is already working.

Pray: *O God, I am discouraged and overwhelmed. I cannot see a way out of my seemingly hopeless situation. I pray that You open my eyes to the ways You are already working in my life so that I can see Your providential care for me. Help me remember that You have a plan, You have an army, and You have my needs in mind.*

DAY 41

SAVE US, O LORD OUR GOD

Now, O Lord *our God, rescue us from his power; then all the kingdoms of the earth will know that you alone, O* Lord*, are God.* (2 Kings 19:19 NLT)

Read: 2 Kings 19:14–37

Have you ever been afraid in the face of a threat? Perhaps you have been mocked by someone who doesn't love the Lord. Remember that even in hardship, God is with us.

Hezekiah was a good king in Judah, doing what was right in the eyes of the Lord. He destroyed the idols of the people, removed pagan worship sites, and led his people to follow God. In return, God blessed Hezekiah.

Eventually, though, King Sennacherib of Assyria laid siege to Jerusalem. Imagine being surrounded by a mighty army while the food and water stores in your walled city slowly run out. That is exactly the situation Hezekiah found himself in.

To make matters worse, Sennacherib's servant, the Rabshakeh, publicly mocked God, telling Hezekiah not to put his trust in the Lord. He claimed that Sennacherib would be victorious because Hezekiah had destroyed the high places and altars where people worshipped God. In their arrogance, the wicked Assyrians were actually the ones sinning against God.

Yet Hezekiah was still in trouble, and his city was still besieged, so he went to the prophet Isaiah and asked him to pray. Then King Sennacherib sent a letter to Hezekiah. Again, he mocked God and mocked Hezekiah's trust in God.

This time, Hezekiah prayed. After praising God, he asked God to listen to him, see his predicament, and save the people of Judah for His own glory, so that others would know that He is God. Before miraculously rescuing His people, God answered Hezekiah through Isaiah, speaking against Sennacherib:

> *Whom have you been defying and ridiculing? Against whom did you raise your voice? At whom did you look with such haughty eyes? It was the Holy One of Israel!*
>
> (2 Kings 19:22 NLT)

Like Hezekiah, believers today can go straight to God for deliverance. Romans 8:38–39 (NLT) tells us:

> *And I am convinced that nothing can ever separate us from God's love. Neither death nor life, neither angels nor demons, neither our fears for today nor our worries about tomorrow—not even the powers of hell can separate us from God's love. No power in the sky above or in the earth below—indeed, nothing in all creation will ever be able to separate us from the love of God that is revealed in Christ Jesus our Lord.*

When you go to our Lord in prayer, you have nothing to fear—not even death—because if you love Jesus and follow Him, you will spend all eternity with Him. Nothing, not even an evil king and his army, can separate you from God's love.

Pray: *O Lord God, You rescued the people of Israel when the angel of the Lord struck down one hundred eighty-five thousand soldiers in the middle of the night. I don't need to be afraid. You are with me. Nothing can separate me from Your love through Christ Jesus. Help me to be courageous and let me always come to You in prayer when I am in need.*

DAY 42

IF I PERISH

Go, gather all the Jews to be found in Susa, and hold a fast on my behalf, and do not eat or drink for three days, night or day. I and my young women will also fast as you do. Then I will go to the king, though it is against the law, and if I perish, I perish. (Esther 4:16)

Read: Esther 3:13–15; 4:1–17

Have you ever rushed into action in the midst of a terrible situation? Maybe you neglected to first seek God's help in prayer. Perhaps you have forgotten that it is God who delivers us.

Going to God is often not our first response, but it is the correct one. Paul writes, *"Do not be anxious about anything, but in everything by prayer and supplication with thanksgiving let your requests be made known to God"* (Philippians 4:6). Not only did Esther pray before jumping into action, but she also asked her fellow Jews in Susa, the capital city of Persia, to pray and fast as well.

King Ahasuerus of Persia ruled a huge kingdom, covering parts of the Middle East, Turkey, Greece, Egypt, and India. After the king angrily kicked his original queen, Vashti, out of the kingdom, he gathered up the beautiful young girls from across the land to become part of his harem. Ahasuerus was taken with Esther, and he made her queen, yet their marriage was anything but a partnership. In fact, it must have been terribly difficult for Esther. She was queen by virtue of being

Ahasuerus's favorite concubine. The only choice she was able to make in the matter was to keep her identity as a Jew hidden.

The situation worsened when Esther's older cousin, Mordecai, told her Ahasuerus had ordered that Jews be killed throughout the empire. Mordecai asked Esther to go to the king for help. Faced with the impending eradication of her people, Esther could have refused to risk her own safety to help. She could have rushed to the king to demand he spare her people. Instead, Esther wisely fasted and prayed for three days with her attendants. She asked Mordecai to gather the Jews in Susa to fast as well.

Approaching the king without an invitation was punishable by death. Yet when Esther went to the king, he held out his scepter and she was safe. In the end, God spared the Jews from extinction when King Ahasuerus sent an order allowing them to fight anyone who attacked them.

Like Esther, our first response to true danger should be to seek God's help. Her prayer wasn't a quick plea, offered as she ran to be the hero of her own story. Instead, she enlisted others to spend three days and nights fasting and praying. Their only focus was their great God whom they were petitioning. God sometimes places His people in a position to act in their own defense against those who hate them. Before acting, we do well to seek God's deliverance in prayer.

Pray: *Dear God, when I am under attack from those who hate You, I am anxious. I also find myself driven to act. I know that my first response to danger must be to seek You in prayer with thanksgiving. Thank You for hearing my requests. Deliver me, O Lord.*

DAY 43

I CALL TO YOU, O LORD

To you, O Lord, I call. For fire has devoured the pastures of the wilderness, and flame has burned all the trees of the field. (Joel 1:19)

Read: Joel 1:13–20

Have you ever heard someone suggest that a disaster or national misfortune, such as war or famine, may be a judgment from God? The book of Joel is a prophecy about God's judgment on rebellious nations. Sometimes God does warn us of His coming judgment so we will turn to Him for rescue.

In the Old Testament books of the prophets, God calls people to repent for three main issues: false gods, false worship, and false justice. Because God is God, we must only worship Him. Nothing can come before our love of God. Also, because God is God, we must worship Him the way He tells us to worship Him. Last, because God is God, we must love and care for the widows, the orphans, the sojourners, and the poor. We don't treat people preferentially because of their position in life.

God gave Joel a prophecy about a coming series of judgments because the people refused to worship God alone, in God's way, or to love God's people. First, there would be a swarm of locusts. Next, there would be drought. Finally, there would be an attack by a great army. There would be pain and devastation, hunger, thirst, and death.

Joel offered the people of Israel a solution from God:

> *Consecrate a fast; call a solemn assembly. Gather the elders and all the inhabitants of the land to the house of the* Lord *your God, and cry out to the* Lord. (Joel 1:14)

Joel himself cried out to God. Then, he prophesied:

> *"Now, therefore," says the* Lord, *"turn to Me with all your heart, with fasting, with weeping, and with mourning." So rend your heart, and not your garments; return to the* Lord *your God, for He is gracious and merciful, slow to anger, and of great kindness; and He relents from doing harm.* (Joel 2:12–13 NKJV)

Sometimes, God allows us to go through hard circumstances as a measure of grace so that we have the opportunity and the motivation to return to Him. As a kind Father, God loves us enough to warn us when we have gone astray. That is a gift we cannot ignore.

Understanding how God deals with us should bring peace. God answers our prayers because of His character, not because of ours. God is gracious, compassionate, slow to anger, and abounding in mercy. God is consistently good and always patient. While we should not speak for the Lord and declare every hardship a judgment, we should be aware that sometimes God warns us with a little pain so we can follow Him away from a lot of pain later.

Pray: *Lord, it seems that disaster is upon us. I call to You because You are gracious, compassionate, and slow to anger. You, Lord, abound in mercy and You relent of catastrophe when we repent. Help me worship You alone in the way You instruct us to worship You. Help me to love and serve others well.*

DAY 44

DELIVER ME FROM TEMPTATION

On reaching the place, he said to them, "Pray that you will not fall into temptation." (Luke 22:40 NIV)

Read: Luke 22:39–46

Do certain situations trigger an automatic reaction for you? Maybe praying for your own spiritual strength is a struggle. Thankfully, we serve a God who delivers us from temptation.

As believers, we all must fight against turning away from Jesus and turning toward our own solutions in life. In the last sentence of the Lord's Prayer, Jesus prayed, *"And lead us not into temptation, but deliver us from evil"* (Matthew 6:13).

Jesus instructed us to seek God's strength when things are going well. So we pray for strength for times when we are more likely to fall into sin—when things are not going according to plan or when we are weak.

The last night of His life, Jesus celebrated the Passover dinner with His disciples. He instituted the Lord's Supper, a remembrance of Jesus's love and sacrifice for believers. Then the disciples argued over who among them would be the greatest, and Simon Peter declared he was ready to go to prison and even death for Jesus. Jesus told Peter that he would, in fact, deny knowing Jesus. However, the Lord had just reassured him, *"But I have prayed for you, Simon, that your faith may not fail. And when you have turned back, strengthen your brothers"* (Luke 22:32 NIV).

Finally, Jesus led His disciples to the Mount of Olives to pray. It was late, and the disciples were probably tired. Yet Jesus told them, *"Pray that you will not fall into temptation"* (Luke 22:40 NIV). That's when Jesus walked a short distance away and knelt to pray. The disciples probably could hear Him praying, yet they gave into the temptation to sleep. Even Peter, who knew he would fail Jesus, slept. While they snored, Jesus prayed, *"Father, if you are willing, take this cup from me; yet not my will, but yours be done"* (Luke 22:42 NIV).

Remember, Jesus knew the horror He was about to endure on our behalf. He knew He would be tried, humiliated, whipped, and beaten, then finally crucified for all to witness. Through His crucifixion, Jesus took the punishment for the sin of all who believe in Him. Being fully God, Jesus was qualified to do this. Being fully human, He asked God to consider releasing Him from the dreaded task. Still, Jesus submitted to God's will. He was crucified for our sin, raised from the dead, and ascended to heaven. One day, He will return for His people so that we can live with Him for all eternity.

Even Jesus's closest friends were subject to their own fears, failings, and temptations. Today, we share the same struggles. Yet we serve a God who delivers us from temptation when we ask Him. If you find yourself struggling to overcome your own selfish desires, ask God to deliver you. Like Jesus did, ask for God's will to be done in your life. The Lord is faithful to hear our need for strength to resist temptation, even before it occurs.

Pray: *Lord, help me to pray for my own spiritual strength. Please deliver me from temptation, from sin, and from evil. Help me to bring You honor and glory. Let Your will be done in my life.*

DAY 45

I WILL BOAST IN MY WEAKNESS

But he said to me, "My grace is sufficient for you, for my power is made perfect in weakness." Therefore I will boast all the more gladly of my weaknesses, so that the power of Christ may rest upon me. (2 Corinthians 12:9)

Read: 2 Corinthians 12:1–10

Have you earnestly pleaded with God to deliver you from a weakness in your life? Perhaps you are facing an illness or challenge that is too big for you to overcome. Do not worry, for we serve a strong God.

The church at Corinth was a particularly challenging body of believers. A group of teachers there opposed Paul's leadership, teaching believers that if Paul was truly being used by the Holy Spirit as an apostle for Jesus, he would be healthy, wealthy, and, well, not Paul. So Paul reluctantly wrote that he was a better servant of Christ than his detractors. For the sake of the gospel, Paul had been whipped, beaten, stoned, shipwrecked, stranded in the sea overnight, imprisoned, and near death. (See 2 Corinthians 11:23–27.)

Paul's opponents also claimed a closer relationship with the Holy Spirit. So Paul shared that he had been taken into heaven, to the paradise where God dwells. There he saw and heard things he was not allowed to repeat. In fact, Paul even humbly wrote about himself in the third person. (See 2 Corinthians 12:1–4.)

Paul sacrificed for the sake of Christ, rather than boasting about his undeniable service to God for the sake of the gospel or about the vision God gave him, writing, *"If I must boast, I will boast of the things that show my weakness"* (2 Corinthians 11:30). Paul had no desire to exalt himself—he only wanted to lift up Jesus. So he shared that God gave him a thorn in the flesh to keep him humble.

Paul tells us he asked God three times to take away the thorn in his flesh that tormented him. God answered Paul, not with a *yes* or a miracle, but with a clear *no*. Paul writes, *"But he said to me, 'My grace is sufficient for you, for my power is made perfect in weakness'"* (2 Corinthians 12:9).

Why doesn't Paul describe his thorn to us? Maybe the nature of the thorn doesn't matter. Instead, we should understand that God allowed Paul to suffer so that Jesus's power would be evident in Paul's life. It was only through the grace of God that Paul was able to share the gospel and establish and strengthen church bodies everywhere he went.

Paul's opponents were wrong. We do not have to be healthy, wealthy, or even wise to serve Jesus in His kingdom. Instead, we must be willing to boast in our weakness so that Jesus's strength and glory shines through. We are called to lay aside our concern for our own glory and exalt Jesus over all else.

Pray: *Lord, Your grace is sufficient for me. Your power is perfected in my weakness. Please remove the thorn in my flesh and give me relief from Satan's torment. If Your answer is "yes," help me serve You without being conceited or exalting myself. Every good trait I have is a gift from You. If Your answer is "no," let me glorify You while I look to You for endurance and comfort.*

PRAYERS OF LAMENT

I have told you all this so that you may have peace in me. Here on earth you will have many trials and sorrows. But take heart, because I have overcome the world.
—John 16:33 NLT

We bring our sorrow to God, our Comforter.

DAY 46

WHY, LORD?

So Moses returned to the Lord *and said, "Lord, why have You brought trouble on this people? Why is it You have sent me? For since I came to Pharaoh to speak in Your name, he has done evil to this people; neither have You delivered Your people at all."* (Exodus 5:22–23 NKJV)

Read: Exodus 5

Have you ever hesitated to tell God how you are feeling? Perhaps you didn't want to complain or seem ungrateful for all the good things the Lord has given you. The Bible, though, is full of lament. In times of grief, overload, and pain, we are to bring our sorrow to God and share it with Him as a child does with a loving Father.

In the days before the exodus, God heard the cry of the Israelite people who were enslaved in Egypt. His answer was to send Moses to act as His agent of rescue. So Moses and his brother, Aaron, traveled to Egypt and gathered all the elders of Israel, explaining to them that the Lord would free them from slavery and give them a new home in the land of Canaan. After the people saw the signs performed by Moses and Aaron, they believed God's words and worshipped Him for hearing their prayers. But Pharaoh responded to Moses's request that God's people be allowed to worship God in the wilderness by making the people's work harder and more miserable. The Israelite leaders reacted by complaining against Moses and Aaron rather than praying to God.

Moses, who had spoken to God in the burning bush and performed God-given miraculous signs, promptly forgot that God promised He would deliver His people and that Pharaoh would initially rebel. So Moses approached God and demanded that He explain why He brought trouble on the Israelites. Why had He sent Moses to speak for God? In fact, Moses said, God hadn't delivered His people at all. Things were actually worse.

This was not the ideal way to pray. Moses promptly forgot the promises of God. Instead, he complained to the Creator of the universe. Moses demanded to know why he was suffering.

Yet God did not respond to Moses in anger or frustration. Instead, God restated that He is the Lord. He had made promises to the ancestors of the Israelites that He intended to keep. He heard their groans and He would rescue them. "*I will take you as My people, and I will be your God. Then you shall know that I am the Lord your God who brings you out from under the burdens of the Egyptians*" (Exodus 6:7 NKJV).

God wants to hear about our sorrow, even when we do not pray the right way. He is our Father who loves His children. When life is hard, our first response should always be to bring our complaints to God. That is the first step to a lament, but it should not be the last part of our prayer of lament.

Pray: *Lord, You are my God, and I am one of Your people. Thank You that I can share my pain and my sorrow with You. Help me remember Your promises to me. Help me also remember Your great love for all who belong to You.*

DAY 47

BLESSED BE THE NAME OF THE LORD

And he said, "Naked I came from my mother's womb, and naked shall I return. The Lord *gave, and the* Lord *has taken away; blessed be the name of the* Lord*."* (Job 1:21)

Read: Job 1

Have you ever struggled to respond righteously to calamity? Perhaps you wonder why God allows you to suffer when you are following Jesus. Yet God uses our suffering for our good and His glory.

The book of Job gives us unique insight into the throne room of heaven. There, God tells Satan that Job is a righteous man. Because Job belongs to the Lord, Satan must receive permission from God to test Job. Surprisingly, God allows Satan to test Job but protects Job's life.

In one day, Job loses his servants, his animals, and his ten beloved children. For an unbeliever, the natural response to this overwhelming sorrow might be to take the suggestion of Job's wife: "*Curse God and die*" (Job 2:9). Job, though, loves the Lord and he knows that not one thing happens in our lives that our sovereign God has not ordained. While that may feel like a hard truth, it is a comfort to remember that our loving, good God is in control and we can trust Him.

Later, after Satan afflicts Job with painful boils, Job asks his bitter wife, "*Shall we receive good from God, and shall we not receive evil?*" (Job 2:10). Often, we are eager to accept God's good blessings, but we struggle to cope when God disciplines us or tests our faith. When Job suffers, his righteous response is to lament. Job submits to God's test of his faith and he worships God.

Job's righteous response in the face of suffering shows his submission to God. Thousands of years later, his prayer models for us how we can lament without sinning or charging God with wrongdoing. God gives and God takes away, yet we still praise the holy name of the Lord.

James 1:2–4 tells us, "*Count it all joy, my brothers, when you meet trials of various kinds, for you know that the testing of your faith produces steadfastness. And let steadfastness have its full effect, that you may be perfect and complete, lacking in nothing.*" When we lament, we bring our sorrows to our caring God. We can also rejoice in each trial, remembering that when God tests our faith, it produces steadfastness, which helps perfect and complete our faith.

God hears, and cares about, our pain and our sorrow. Our prayers often bring change to our situation because God often answers us when we go to Him with our concerns. Yet ultimately, He is the Lord and His purposes may be beyond our understanding. We can submit to His will for our lives, knowing He is working to grow our faith—our trust—in Him.

Pray: *Lord, let me worship You even in my pain. I arrived in this world with nothing, and I will leave without possessions. Lord, You gave and You have taken away. Blessed be Your name. Let me rejoice when You test my faith. Thank You for producing steadfastness in me so that I will receive the crown of life.*

DAY 48

MY SOUL IS TROUBLED

Return, O Lord, and rescue me. Save me because of your unfailing love. (Psalm 6:4 NLT)

Read: Psalm 6

Have you ever been through a situation you felt might end your life? Perhaps you were dealing with an illness or accident, a dangerous person, or a devastating personal loss you were not sure you could survive. In times of trouble, a lament is the right kind of Bible prayer to our loving and kind God.

A lament is a structured prayer in which the person praying shares her pain and sorrow with God. She asks God for help and then she proclaims trust in His help. Because she knows God will hear her prayer, a lament often includes praise.

In Psalm 6, David laments a painful circumstance he fears may be the result of his own sin. He seeks God, praying, "*O Lord, rebuke me not in your anger, nor discipline me in your wrath*" (verse 1). During his life, David's sin certainly did create some painful consequences. For instance, as a result of David summoning Bathsheba to his room and then arranging for the death of her husband, Uriah, David's first child with Bathsheba died.

So David asks God for mercy and grace. Then, he asks God to rescue him because it is in keeping with God's good character, His loving-kindness. David also wants to continue to bring glory to God through his worship. He writes, "*For in death there is no remembrance of you; in Sheol who will give you praise?*" (Psalm 6:5).

After sharing his agony and grief with God again, David declares his trust in God. He knows that God has heard him. God will receive David's prayer, and He will protect David from his enemies.

Our sorrow is not always the result of our own sin. Sometimes, we must endure a test designed to grow our faith in God. Other times, pain is the result of living in a fallen and corrupted world. Occasionally we suffer the consequences of someone else's sinful act.

There are times, too, when God uses our lives to bring glory to Himself. This was the case in John 9, when Jesus healed a blind man. His disciples asked whether the man's sin or his parents' sin caused his blindness. *"Jesus answered, 'It was not that this man sinned, or his parents, but that the works of God might be displayed in him'"* (John 9:3).

The lament is a wonderful framework in which we humbly approach God in our pain. Rather than complaining against God's will for our lives, we share our complaints over our circumstances with God. We ask Him for help, pour out our pain before Him, confess our belief in God's willingness to help us, and then praise Him for His wonderful character.

Pray: *Lord, let me always turn to You in my distress. Be gracious to me and rescue my soul. Save me because of Your loving-kindness. Let me serve and praise You. I am overcome with grief, but You have heard my prayer and will answer me in Your goodness. I am protected from all who wish to harm me in my weakness. Praise the holy name of God!*

DAY 49

HOPE IN GOD

Why, my soul, are you downcast? Why so disturbed within me? Put your hope in God, for I will yet praise him, my Savior and my God. (Psalm 42:11 NIV)

Read: Psalm 42

Have you ever felt separated from God? Jesus felt that way as well. Because Jesus has lived our pain, He is our High Priest who understands us when we pray.

Just like a deer runs through a field, longing for water, we thirst for the presence of God when we feel He is distant from us. In times of trouble, we may find that people mock God, asking us where God is in our lives. Or they may taunt our faith, asking us why we are not seeking God. We may even wistfully remember joyful times when God answered our prayers.

The author of Psalm 42 asks God why he is depressed and in turmoil before reminding himself to put his hope in God. But he will continue to praise his Savior, no matter how he is feeling. He remembers that God will, in fact, answer him:

By day the LORD directs his love, at night his song is with me—a prayer to the God of my life. (Psalm 42:8 NIV)

We all have times when we feel depressed, anxious, or as though God is far from us. Yet God is not afraid of our emotions. He is not overwhelmed by our pain. God created us to experience a broad spectrum of feelings. When Jesus came to earth, He felt them too. We can go to Jesus with our emotional turmoil precisely because He understands our weakness and He is willing to offer us mercy and grace.

Hebrews 4:14–16 says:

> *Since then we have a great high priest who has passed through the heavens, Jesus, the Son of God, let us hold fast our confession. For we do not have a high priest who is unable to sympathize with our weaknesses, but one who in every respect has been tempted as we are, yet without sin. Let us then with confidence draw near to the throne of grace, that we may receive mercy and find grace to help in time of need.*

Jesus is our great High Priest, the Son of God. He is sympathetic to our weakness—though He lived His life on earth without ever sinning. As Christians, we can go boldly to Jesus on His throne of grace. He is ready and willing to hear us and to offer us mercy and grace. You may not always feel your fellowship with God through Jesus, but you can be assured that Jesus is always available to you if you love Him and seek Him out.

Pray: *God, I am thirsty for Your presence. I am overcome with my own feelings, with anxiety, depression, and turmoil. Yet I will put my hope in God. I will still praise You, Jesus, my Savior and my God. I will approach the throne of grace with boldness because You have compassion on my weakness. You will answer my thirst for You with waterfalls of Your presence. I will see Your faithful love day and night. Your song in me will be my prayer to You, the God of my life.*

DAY 50
I AM IN DISTRESS

See, O Lord, that I am in distress; my soul is troubled; my heart is overturned within me, for I have been very rebellious. Outside the sword bereaves, at home it is like death. (Lamentations 1:20 NKJV)

Read: Lamentations 1:20–22

Have you ever disciplined a child, motivated by your love for them? Maybe your child acted spitefully toward a sibling, and you took away their toys for the day. Just as we discipline our children for their own good, God also disciplines us.

Hebrews 12:7–11 tells us to be glad when God disciplines or chastens us because it means He is treating us as His children. The passage ends with, *"Now no chastening seems to be joyful for the present, but painful; nevertheless, afterward it yields the peaceable fruit of righteousness to those who have been trained by it"* (Hebrews 12:11 NKJV).

The book of Lamentations is a long lament to God following the end of the exile of Judah to Babylon. Throughout the books of the prophets, God sent messengers to warn the people of Israel and Judah to turn from idolatry and worship only Him. He cautioned His people to worship Him in the way He had instructed them. Over and over, God reminded His people to love the widows, the orphans, the poor, and the sojourners. Yet God's people repeatedly rebelled and did what was right in their own eyes.

So God disciplined His people. In order to bring them back to Him, God allowed Babylon to destroy Jerusalem. The people of God were led away to a distant land to serve a pagan king. It was a bleak time for them.

So the author of Lamentations laments, describing the terrible pain of the exile. Then he remembers where his hope comes from. Even in their darkest hour, God's people are not without a source of comfort, mercy, and joy. That is because our hope is never in our own goodness or in our own faith. Our hope is always in the character of our God. Lamentations 3:22–26 (NKJV) says:

> *Through the LORD's mercies we are not consumed, because His compassions fail not. They are new every morning; great is Your faithfulness. "The LORD is my portion," says my soul, "therefore I hope in Him!" The LORD is good to those who wait for Him, to the soul who seeks Him. It is good that one should hope and wait quietly for the salvation of the LORD.*

Even in the worst of circumstances, our Father God is faithful. He is always working for our good and for His glory. Our God is always good, always just, and always steadfast. You can trust our Father in all situations because He is the same yesterday, today, and tomorrow.

Pray: *Oh, Lord, I am in distress and I am troubled. I have been rebellious against You. Yet I know that You discipline me because I am Your child. Lord, Your steadfast love and compassion never fail. Your mercies never come to an end, and Your faithfulness is great. My hope is in You and I will seek You and wait quietly for Your salvation.*

DAY 51

THE GOD OF ALL GRACE

> *And the God of all grace, who called you to his eternal glory in Christ, after you have suffered a little while, will himself restore you and make you strong, firm and steadfast.*
>
> (1 Peter 5:10 NIV)

Read: 1 Peter 5:6–11

Have you ever suffered or struggled for the sake of Jesus? Perhaps you lost a friend, a family member, or a job because you are a Christian. Even during trials or loss, we can trust our God to restore us.

Peter wrote his first letter to Christians who were suffering persecution for their faith. He begins by teaching us to praise God because He has given us hope through Jesus's resurrection from the dead. In trouble, Peter reminds us:

> *In all this you greatly rejoice, though now for a little while you may have had to suffer grief in all kinds of trials. These have come so that the proven genuineness of your faith—of greater worth than gold, which perishes even though refined by fire—may result in praise, glory and honor when Jesus Christ is revealed.* (1 Peter 1:6–7 NIV)

Peter ends his letter by reminding us to live humbly before God. He warns us, too, to be wary, describing our enemy Satan as a hungry lion *"looking for someone to devour"* (1 Peter 5:8 NIV). We can take comfort in the fact that God cares for and strengthens Christians everywhere who are also struggling because of their faith.

When it seems too hard to suffer for your faith, remember the promise of Revelation 21:3–4 (NIV):

> *And I heard a loud voice from the throne saying, "Look! God's dwelling place is now among the people, and he will dwell with them. They will be his people, and God himself will be with them and be their God. 'He will wipe every tear from their eyes. There will be no more death' or mourning or crying or pain, for the old order of things has passed away."*

Though we lament in our trials, we can rejoice because when we turn to God as our strength in times of trouble, our faith is shown to be real. When Jesus returns, all praise, glory, and honor will belong to Him. And since we are His, Christians will share in eternity with Him.

Our suffering on this earth is short-lived. One day, we will live on the new earth with Jesus and He will give us new, glorified, eternal bodies. Then God will restore us and make us strong, firm, and steadfast. Our hope is in God. He is full of grace, eternal, and the God of all power.

Pray: *Lord, help me rejoice in my trials. They will last only for a little while, and You have used them to prove the genuineness of my faith and to bring all praise, glory, and honor to Jesus. Help me humble myself under Your mighty hand and cast all my anxiety on You. Let my mind be alert and sober so I can resist the devil and stand firm in the faith. Help me to faithfully remember my suffering fellow believers across the globe in prayer. One day You will restore me and make me strong, firm, and steadfast.*

DAY 52

HOW LONG, LORD?

They cried out with a loud voice, "O Sovereign Lord, holy and true, how long before you will judge and avenge our blood on those who dwell on the earth?" (Revelation 6:10)

Read: Revelation 6:9–11

Have you ever witnessed a great injustice against a believer and wondered how the Lord could allow the crime to go unpunished? We rarely see martyrdom today, but over the centuries and throughout the world, many people have died for the sake of the gospel. However, we can trust that our God is truly just.

The fifth seal in Revelation gives us a vision of the souls of those martyred for preaching the Word of God or for claiming Christ as their Savior. They are praying to God from under the altar in heaven. The souls ask God how long it will be before He judges those who killed them. How long until God avenges them, punishing the wicked on earth?

After their plea, these martyrs are each given a white robe. They lived as victorious witnesses to Jesus, giving everything they had to the Lord. Now their souls are pure as snow and they are forgiven. The martyrs are told to rest just a little longer, for God has determined exactly which souls will join their number, and it isn't quite time for the Lord to judge.

Today, we may be squeamish about the idea of God judging the earth. Yet if someone we love is injured intentionally, we want to see the person who hurt them stand in court before a just judge. God has promised that He is both just, and He is our

Judge. One day, He will bring justice to all people. That is good news; it should not upset us.

In Romans 12:19–21, Paul writes, "*Beloved, never avenge yourselves, but leave it to the wrath of God, for it is written, 'Vengeance is mine, I will repay, says the Lord.' To the contrary, 'if your enemy is hungry, feed him; if he is thirsty, give him something to drink; for by so doing you will heap burning coals on his head.' Do not be overcome by evil, but overcome evil with good.*"

When we witness injustice against believers, we can earnestly ask God, "How long before You judge those who are hurting us?" That, too, is a form of lament. In one question, we are telling the Lord about the injustice we see and acknowledging that we trust Him as our Judge and our Savior.

One day, God will bring His children into the new earth to live with Him forever. Those who have rejected Him will be judged by the fair and just Judge of all the earth. You can thank God that He will make all things right in the end.

Pray: *Lord, I see injustice in the world against those who love and serve You. My soul cries out, "O Sovereign Lord, holy and true, how long before You will judge? How long before You avenge the blood of the martyrs?" Help me to wait just a little while longer. While I do, help me remember to pray for the persecuted church. Please grant repentance to those who are persecuting Your people so they, too, may come to salvation in You. Let me overcome evil with good.*

PRAYERS OF GUIDANCE

For You are my rock and my fortress; therefore, for Your name's sake, lead me and guide me.
—Psalm 31:3 (NKJV)

We ask for God's help in determining His will for our lives.

DAY 53

WHY IS THIS HAPPENING?

But the two children struggled with each other in her womb. So she went to ask the Lord *about it. "Why is this happening to me?" she asked.* (Genesis 25:22 NLT)

Read: Genesis 25:19–28

Have you ever wondered why something is occurring in your life? Maybe an event seems out of character with your devotion to God and to your family. Yet God always has a plan.

God's calling on Rebekah's life was clear, so it is no surprise that she went straight to Him when she didn't understand what was happening with her unborn children. When Abraham's son, Isaac, was forty years old, Abraham sent his servant to find a godly wife for him rather than choosing a pagan woman from the surrounding countryside. Abraham's servant asked God to make his choice for Isaac's wife clear. God answered the servant's prayer, and Rebekah was shown to be God's chosen wife for Isaac. (See Genesis 24:12–27.)

After they were married, Rebekah was unable to have children. Isaac prayed for her, and God answered again, blessing Rebekah with a pregnancy. Over time, Rebekah felt that whatever was occurring in her womb was not right. We know that she was pregnant with twins, but she likely had no idea. Instead, Rebekah knew she was uncomfortable. While the end of pregnancy can feel miserable, Rebekah's twins were painfully warring within her. In fact, they were fighting even during their birth. Jacob's arrival followed Esau's, and he was born with his little hand firmly clenched around Esau's heel.

The brothers' personalities were developed before they were ever born. The firstborn Esau, who should have inherited nearly everything from Isaac, was careless and nonchalant about his role as the eldest brother and family heir. Jacob, later called Israel, was deceptive, cunning, and determined to take his brother's position. Indeed, when Rebekah asked God why she was suffering, the Lord shared that there were two separate nations, or people groups, fighting in her womb. One would be stronger than the other, and the oldest would serve the youngest. (See Genesis 25:23.)

Throughout the Bible, there are prayers asking God for guidance, wisdom, and discernment. Over and over, Scripture reassures us that God has a good plan and we can seek His direction. For instance, Proverbs 3:5–6 (NLT) says: "*Trust in the Lord with all your heart; do not depend on your own understanding. Seek his will in all you do, and he will show you which path to take.*"

Life is often quite unpredictable. It is not unusual, even when you belong to Jesus, to wonder why something is occurring in your life. Because you know that God plans the events of your life, you can absolutely go to Him as Rebekah did and ask, "*Why is this happening to me?*"

Pray: *Lord, help me always to come straight to You when I question the events of my life. Thank You for the story of Rebekah, in which I clearly see Your hand guiding her life. Please help me understand why this thing is happening to me. Please give me peace and help me trust You with all my heart. I don't want to depend on my own understanding. I want to seek Your will in all that I do, knowing You will show me the right direction to go.*

DAY 54

KEEP ME FROM EVIL

Jabez called upon the God of Israel, saying, "Oh that you would bless me and enlarge my border, and that your hand might be with me, and that you would keep me from harm so that it might not bring me pain!" And God granted what he asked. (1 Chronicles 4:10)

Read: 1 Chronicles 4:9–10

Have you ever worried that a choice someone else made on your behalf might impact your life in a negative way? Perhaps you have a specific concern about your life because of the choices you have seen occur through the generations of your family. You can ask God to protect you, just as Jabez did.

In ancient Jewish culture, names were a big deal. They were often connected to a description of how the child came into the world. Names could also communicate a parent's hopes for a child or even feelings about the newborn baby's personality. God sometimes named or renamed people in Scripture to communicate a message about Himself or His purpose for their life. Proverbs 22:1 says, *"A good name is to be chosen rather than great riches."*

The brief story of Jabez's life and prayer appears in a list of names of the male descendants of Judah, one of the twelve sons of Jacob. Jabez's name in Hebrew means "he causes pain," so he apparently was named by his mother after an especially painful childbirth. The man must have been somewhat dismayed that his mother named him Pain.

So when Jabez went to the Lord in prayer, he asked God to bless him. Jabez asked for God's care and attention. He asked the Lord to give him land, so that he could make a living. Then, Jabez asked God to keep him from harm—to keep pain far from him. In four ways, Jabez asked God to guide him in a way that would keep him from his very namesake, pain.

We should not interpret Jabez's prayer as a case in which he presented to God his desire for his own good in just the right word order. Nor should we conclude that God is superstitious about names. Rather, we learn that an honorable man went to the Lord with his anxiety. Jabez asked God to do good to him, and God granted his request.

Jesus had this to say about our worries:

> *Come to me, all you who are weary and burdened, and I will give you rest. Take my yoke upon you and learn from me, for I am gentle and humble in heart, and you will find rest for your souls. For my yoke is easy and my burden is light.* (Matthew 11:28–30 NIV)

What a relief it is that Jesus cares about your worries. You can go to Him and find comfort, blessing, and direction for your life.

Pray: *Jesus, I praise You for You are gentle and humble in heart. I am weary and heavy-laden, but I know You will give me rest. Your burden is light. Help me, please, to be honorable before You. I ask that You bless me in life and in work and with my family. Please provide for me and those I love and keep me from harm and from pain.*

DAY 55

GIVE ME WISDOM AND KNOWLEDGE

Give me wisdom and knowledge, that I may lead this people, for who is able to govern this great people of yours?
(2 Chronicles 1:10 NIV)

Read: 2 Chronicles 1:1–13

Have you ever played the game where you imagine being granted just one wish and then you name the one thing you would wish for? It is a game that can make us feel clever, but it can also expose our hearts. After all, do we want material gain for our own use, or do we want to be equipped to steward our lives to the honor and glory of our wise God?

When David's son, Solomon, became king of all of Israel, God came to him in the night and gave him the chance to expose his heart, telling Solomon to ask Him for whatever he wanted. In response, Solomon praised God for showing kindness to David and for making Solomon king after his father's death. Then he asked for wisdom and knowledge so that he could lead God's people well.

Indeed, leading a nation to the glory of God would be an exceedingly difficult task. It is hard enough to get all the kids in the car with everyone's shoes on their feet. Solomon well understood what he later wrote in Proverbs 16:16 (NIV): *"How much better to get wisdom than gold, to get insight rather than silver!"*

Rather than asking for wealth, possessions, honor, health and longevity, or even revenge, Solomon asked for help stewarding God's people. For that reason, God gave Solomon wisdom and knowledge. Then, He promised to also give him immense wealth, possessions, and honor.

Ephesians 5:15–16 (NIV) tells us, "*Be very careful, then, how you live—not as unwise but as wise, making the most of every opportunity, because the days are evil. Therefore do not be foolish, but understand what the Lord's will is.*" We do well to seek wisdom from God so we can understand His will for our lives. In fact, we need God's wisdom just as we need the food we eat or the air we breathe.

Though none of us are governing a vast people group or stewarding the riches of a nation, we can still go to God and ask for His help to accomplish the tasks He puts before us. Whatever the Lord has called you to—whether it is marriage, parenting, ministering to others, or showing hospitality to your neighbors—He will equip you when you ask for wisdom and guidance. For God has given every believer a life and resources to steward wisely to His glory.

Pray: *Wise Father, thank You for all You have given me to care for in my life. How can I steward those I am responsible for and the resources You have given me without the wisdom and knowledge that comes from You? Please give me wisdom that is better than gold and insight that is more precious than silver. Help me to live as one who is wise, making the most of every opportunity before You. Please give me discernment and knowledge from Your Word, so I will understand Your will.*

DAY 56

NOTHING IS TOO HARD FOR YOU

Ah, Lord God! Behold, You have made the heavens and the earth by Your great power and outstretched arm. There is nothing too hard for You. (Jeremiah 32:17 NKJV)

Read: Jeremiah 32:16–25

Do you sometimes struggle to determine the next right thing to do? Our God works all things for our good and to His glory. We can trust Him because He is the Maker of all things, His character never changes, and He is carrying out His wonderful plan for all of humanity.

During the year-long Babylonian siege on Jerusalem, God instructed Jeremiah to buy land about an hour walk from Jerusalem. God had already revealed to Jeremiah that Jerusalem would fall to the Babylonians, the temple would be destroyed, and the people of Judah would be led off to Babylon. This would happen because the people of Judah had rebelled against God in open sin and idol worship. God patiently called His people back to Him, yet they had refused to repent.

Even though it didn't seem to make sense, Jeremiah bought the land. Then, he praised God, remembering the good deeds of the Lord. He confessed the ongoing sins of the people, finally coming to the Lord with his request for guidance. Jeremiah wanted to know why God directed him to purchase the soon-to-be-conquered land.

What a sweet answer God had for him. God was going to cleanse the land of idols and bring the people to repentance.

Then, He would bring the repentant people of Judah back to the land He had given them. God promised, *"For thus says the Lord: Just as I have brought all this great disaster upon this people, so I will bring upon them all the good that I promise them"* (Jeremiah 32:42). God's direction to buy land was a promise that He would restore Judah one day.

Ephesians 1:11–12 (NIV) says, *"In him we were also chosen, having been predestined according to the plan of him who works out everything in conformity with the purpose of his will, in order that we, who were the first to put our hope in Christ, might be for the praise of his glory."* Our God, who made the heavens and the earth, has a plan for our good and for His glory. We can trust God's plan because He is good.

God is concerned with growing our character and our obedience to Him. The Lord will always be glorified through all events. Not every hardship comes because we are living in willful disobedience to God. When life is tough, though, we want to stop and ask God to show us our sin so that we can turn away from rebellion and turn toward Jesus. We can ask Him, too, to grow our character as we cling to Him.

Pray: *God, thank You for Your grace and mercy. I see Your mercy as You disciplined Your people yet promised to restore them to their land. Make me wise and guide me as I walk through my day. Help me to hear when the words of my mouth do not honor You, the Maker of all things. Prick my conscience when I offend You, Lord, and give me the wisdom and humility to repent and turn toward Jesus.*

DAY 57
THE KNOWER OF HEARTS

And they prayed and said, "You, Lord, who know the hearts of all, show which one of these two you have chosen."
(Acts 1:24)

Read: Acts 1:15–26

When you make an important decision in life, do you ask the Lord for guidance first? Perhaps you seek wisdom in Scripture, then pray. After Jesus was crucified, resurrected, and ascended to heaven, the disciples and members of the early church made a habit of seeking God's will in prayer. They knew that God's purpose always prevails.

At the beginning of His ministry, Jesus chose twelve disciples to be His apostles—close friends who would travel with Him, eat and pray together, and learn from His teachings. When it was time for God's salvation plan to be completed with Jesus paying the debt for our sins on the cross, one of the Twelve, Judas Iscariot, betrayed Jesus. Judas led the chief priests, the Pharisees, and a band of soldiers to the garden where Jesus was praying. This was no mistake. Judas's betrayal was a part of God's salvation plan. After the crucifixion, Judas came to a full realization of his wicked act and rather than repenting, he committed suicide.

The eleven remaining apostles were sent forth to share the gospel and lead the new church. Once the early church began to meet together, about one hundred and twenty sisters and brothers in Christ devoted themselves to regular prayer as a group.

This habit of prayer, no doubt, helped them be receptive to the leading of the Holy Spirit.

When Peter announced that it was time for the group to choose another one of Jesus's followers to replace Judas to become the twelfth apostle, they naturally sought the Lord through prayer. The disciples cast lots, and Matthias became the twelfth apostle. Later, God added other apostles, such as Paul and Barnabas, to their number. While all of the disciples spread the gospel, the apostles specifically were sent on missions to do so.

We do not draw lots today. Rather, we turn to God's Word in the Bible. The Holy Spirit also dwells within our hearts, helping us as we seek to live according to God's plan. Proverbs 19:21 (NIV) states: *"Many are the plans in a person's heart, but it is the LORD's purpose that prevails."*

God has given us His Word, with directions on how to live righteously in a way that honors and glorifies Him. Scripture is a valuable gift to us, helping us understand His will for us and make wise choices. The Holy Spirit is faithful to make us uncomfortable with poor decisions and to put us at peace with good ones. Though God allows us a great deal of freedom in the choices we make in our lives, it is still wise to seek God in prayer before we make important decisions. There are times when our plan may seem good, but God's purpose for our lives is always better.

Pray: *Lord, You know my heart and the hearts of others. I'm faced with an important decision. Please help me choose the path You have for me. I have many plans, but Your purpose will prevail. Help me to live in Your will for me, Lord.*

DAY 58

ROOTED AND GROUNDED IN LOVE

That He would grant you, according to the riches of His glory, to be strengthened with might through His Spirit in the inner man, that Christ may dwell in your hearts through faith; that you, being rooted and grounded in love.

(Ephesians 3:16–17 NKJV)

Read: Ephesians 3:14–21

Do you ever struggle to love fellow Christians? Perhaps you even find it difficult to fathom the immense love Jesus has for you. While loving others may sometimes be a struggle, God strengthens us to love.

Paul wanted us to understand that while we are separated from God by our sin, we are reconciled to Him through the work of Jesus on the cross. Jesus took the punishment for the sins of all who believe in Him and repent. Now believers are forgiven, adopted as children of God and saved by grace through our faith in Jesus.

Not only did God save the Jews who believed in Christ and repented, He saved the gentiles too. We are all one family, the church, united in Christ as one body in the Holy Spirit. Jesus gives each believer gifts of the Holy Spirit, which we use to serve and strengthen the body of Christ and share the gospel with others so that they too may be saved.

In Ephesians, Paul spends three chapters explaining the mystery of the gospel and the love of Jesus. Then, he pivots into another three chapters, explaining how we are to love others as

Jesus loves us. This loving others is not an easy task. In fact, we need to wear spiritual armor to carry out our work for the Lord. So before Paul tells us how to live for Jesus, he prays for us. You can pray this prayer for yourself, for the believers in your life, and for the members of the church throughout the world.

Believers from all nations are joined together through Christ into one family of God. So Paul bows his knees before God the Father, who cares enough for His people to name every family. In his prayer, Paul asks God to strengthen each believer through the power of the Holy Spirit, with Christ dwelling in our hearts.

Paul asks God to help us to be like a tree with our roots firmly planted in love. He asks that we understand the great width, length, depth, and height of this massive reservoir of God's love for us. For if we experience the love of Jesus, then we will be filled with the fullness of God.

Finally, Paul reminds us that God can do far more than we can even think to ask because God's power works in us. Through the church, the united body of Christ, we bring glory to God, and His glory is forever.

Pray: *Father, I confess that sometimes it is hard to love my fellow believers. Yet Jesus paid the price for my sin and for theirs. He has united all believers from all nations throughout time into one body, His church. Help me to be strengthened through the Holy Spirit. Let Jesus dwell in my heart because of my faith in Him. Help me be rooted and grounded in love, so my love for others in Your church will bring glory to You forever.*

DAY 59

ASK GOD FOR WISDOM

If any of you lacks wisdom, let him ask God, who gives generously to all without reproach, and it will be given him. (James 1:5)

Read: James 1:5–8

Have you ever found yourself paralyzed by indecision? Maybe you tend to head decisively down a path, only to question later whether you made a mistake. Perhaps when you read the Bible, you wonder how it applies to your own life. Thankfully, God gives wisdom generously.

The word *wisdom* in the Bible is not just used to indicate knowledge of God and His Word. Wisdom is also the application of that knowledge, the ability to put what you know into practice. In the beginning of the book of Proverbs, King Solomon writes that the proverbs, which are wisdom statements, exist:

> *To teach people wisdom and discipline, to help them understand the insights of the wise. … to teach people to live disciplined and successful lives, to help them do what is right, just, and fair.* (Proverbs 1:2–3 NLT)

As followers of Jesus, we want to know God's wisdom and we desire to understand His Word. We also need to be able to apply God's Word to our lives so that we can live with insight, righteousness, justice, and equity.

In his letter to believers, James tells us that if we find that we lack wisdom in any way, we should go straight to God and ask Him to give it to us. We do this knowing that God answers our prayers because of His character rather than ours. God is generous and gives to all without reproach. This means that no matter how foolish we have been in the past, God won't criticize us when we come to Him to ask for wisdom. Instead, He will give it to us.

James also tells us how we should approach God to ask for wisdom. We must ask in faith, believing in God and His attributes, rather than showing faith in our own ability to have faith. We do not have to hope that we have gathered up enough faith, as one gathers courage to do something truly difficult. Instead, we only have to trust that God is exactly who He says He is. The longer you know God and the more you learn about Him through Scripture, the more He will show you that His character is true.

Later in his letter James writes, "*When you ask, you do not receive, because you ask with wrong motives, that you may spend what you get on your pleasures*" (James 4:3 NIV). Yet when you ask God for wisdom without doubting that God will give it to you, you seek knowledge of God and also understanding of how to apply that wisdom to your life. You do this so that you can live righteously for God, serving others and bringing glory to His name.

Pray: *Dear God, You give generously to all without criticism or reproach. I need wisdom. I want to know who You are and to understand Your will for believers. Please help me apply that knowledge to my life so that I can live to Your glory. I believe You can do all things, and I trust You. Please take away any doubt that hides in my heart. Amen.*

DAY 60

COME, LORD JESUS!

He who testifies to these things says, "Surely I am coming soon." Amen. Come, Lord Jesus! The grace of the Lord Jesus be with all. Amen. (Revelation 22:20–21)

Read: Revelation 22

In your prayers of praise and thanksgiving, do you long to see Jesus? Perhaps during your prayers of confession, supplication, and intercession, you wish for the day when sin and pain will be no more. Maybe you long for a time when there is no need for deliverance or for lament, when your guidance will come directly from Jesus Himself. Jesus is returning!

In the last book and last chapter of God's Word, the apostle John is given a vision of the new Jerusalem on the new earth, where the river of the water of life flows from the throne of God and of the Lamb, who is Jesus. For each person who is made righteous by Jesus's blood, there will be eternal life, infinite health, and a world without sin. We will live in the presence of God, worshipping Him forever.

In this last chapter of the Bible, Jesus promises several times that He is coming soon. He will return to gather His people to live with Him forever. But when is *soon*? Peter writes:

But do not overlook this one fact, beloved, that with the Lord one day is as a thousand years, and a thousand years as one day. The Lord is not slow to fulfill his promise as some count slowness, but is patient toward you, not wishing that any should perish, but that all should reach repentance.

(2 Peter 3:8–9)

We can be assured that Jesus is returning when the time is just right. In Revelation 22:17–20, we see the prayer, "*Come,*" three times. First, the Holy Spirit and the Bride—all believers from all nations throughout all time—call out, "*Come.*" Next, we are told that the one who hears John's words in Revelation ought to say, "*Come*" (verse 17). Then, Jesus declares in verse 20, "*Surely I am coming soon*" and in agreement, John says, "*Amen. Come, Lord Jesus!*"

"*Come, Lord Jesus*" is to be the prayer of our hearts when things are hard and when times are good. It should be our prayer when we are seeking His guidance while we wait for Him. Come, Lord Jesus! Nothing on this earth can compare to life in the presence of our Lord in eternity.

Paul tells us how to wait for Jesus's coming return, writing, "*For the grace of God has appeared, bringing salvation for all people, training us to renounce ungodliness and worldly passions, and to live self-controlled, upright, and godly lives in the present age, waiting for our blessed hope, the appearing of the glory of our great God and Savior Jesus Christ, who gave himself for us to redeem us from all lawlessness and to purify for himself a people for his own possession who are zealous for good works*" (Titus 2:11–14). Amen!

Pray: *Lord, thank You for giving me the water of life without price. I praise You, Jesus, for saving me—redeeming me from lawlessness and purifying me as one of Your people. Thank You for Your guidance in all that I undertake and thank You for coming soon. Come, Lord Jesus! Amen.*